Colombia

Colombia

BY

MARION MORRISON

Enchantment of the World
Second Series

Children's Press®

A Division of Scholastic Inc.

NEW YORK   TORONTO   LONDON   AUCKLAND   SYDNEY
MEXICO CITY   NEW DELHI   HONG KONG
DANBURY, CONNECTICUT

Consultant: Beatriz de la Mora, M.A., Teaching Affiliate, Department of Spanish and Portuguese, Stanford University

Please note: All statistics are as up-to-date as possible at the time of publication.

Book design by Ox+Company, Inc.

Library of Congress Cataloging-in-Publication Data

Morrison, Marion.
 Colombia / by Marion Morrison.
  p. cm. — (Enchantment of the world. Second series)
 Includes bibliographical references (p.) and index.
Summary: Describes the geography, history, economy, natural
resources, culture, religion, and people of the South American
country of Colombia.
 ISBN 0-516-21106-4
1. Colombia—Juvenile literature. [1. Colombia.] I. Title.
II. Series.
F2258.5.M67 1999
918.61—dc21

98-19307
CIP
AC

CHILDREN'S PRESS and associated logos are trademarks and or registered
trademarks of Scholastic Library Publishing. SCHOLASTIC and associated
logos are trademarks and or registered trademarks of Scholastic Inc.
4 5 6 7 8 9 10 R 08 07 06 05 04 03

Acknowledgments

The following people and organizations were especially help-ful in the preparation of this volume. In Santafé de Bogotá, Amalia Low, Nicholas Bright Samper and Alec S. Bright, the Gold Museum and National Library. In London, the library staff at Canning House and the Cultural Office of the Colombian Embassy. In Suffolk, Mike Harding, for his help following a recent journey to some of Colombia's national parks.

Contents

Cover photo:
A historic building
in Cartagena

Bahía Taganga

An iguana

Old Gold, New Gold

Lake Guatavita lies in a hilly region north of Santafé de Bogotá, Colombia's capital. For centuries the lake has attracted explorers and adventurers of all kinds for it is said to be the legendary lake of *El Dorado* (the Gilded Man).

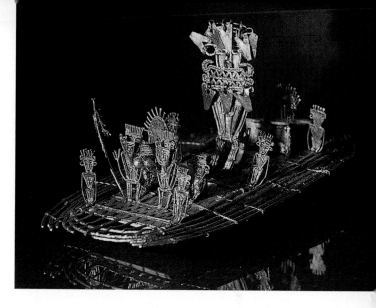

A golden raft depicting the El Dorado ceremony

WHEN THE SPANIARDS ARRIVED IN South America early in the sixteenth century, they heard of a ceremony that took place when there was a new ruler of the Muisca, or Chibcha, people. After he became chief, the new ruler was shut up in a cave. He was not allowed to see women and he was forbidden to use salt. When he was permitted to leave, he made a pilgrimage to Lake Guatavita, where a raft of rushes was prepared with offerings and sacrifices for the gods, and the air was filled with the scent of burning incense.

The chief was stripped of his clothes and covered from head to foot with fine gold dust. His nobles, wearing feathers, crowns, bracelets, earrings, and pendants—all made of gold— then joined him on the raft and placed a great heap of gold and emeralds at his feet. As the raft left the shore, the music of trumpets and flutes sounded across the lake.

In the middle of the lake, the chief and his nobles threw all the gold, emeralds, and other treasures into the water as offerings to their gods, and the chief dived into the water to remove the gold dust from his skin. Eyewitnesses said that then "they returned to the shore, again accompanied by a great fanfare of music, and much singing and dancing."

Opposite: **Lake Guatavita, the legendary lake of El Dorado, may contain a treasure in gold and precious jewels.**

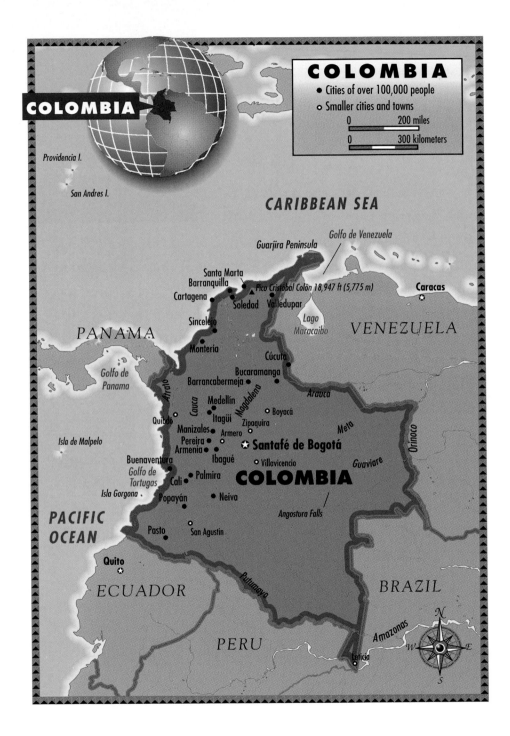

COLOMBIA

COLOMBIA
- • Cities of over 100,000 people
- ○ Smaller cities and towns

0   200 miles

0   300 kilometers

CARIBBEAN SEA

Providencia I.

San Andres I.

Golfo de Venezuela

Guarjira Peninsula

Santa Marta
Barranquilla
Cartagena
Soledad   Valledupar
Pico Cristóbal Colón 18,947 ft (5,775 m)
Caracas

Sincelejo

Lago Maracaibo

VENEZUELA

PANAMA

Montería

Cúcuta

Golfo de Panama

Bucaramanga
Barrancabermeja

Arauca

Atrato

Cauca

Medellín

Magdalena

Boyacá

Meta

Quibdó

Itagüí
Zipaquira

Manizales   Armero
Pereira
Armenia   ☆ **Santafé de Bogotá**

Isla de Malpelo

Orinoco

Buenaventura
Golfo de Tortugas

Ibagué

Villavicencio

Guaviare

Cali   Palmira

COLOMBIA

Isla Gorgona

Popayán   Neiva

**PACIFIC
OCEAN**

Pasto   San Agustín

Angostura Falls

Quito

ECUADOR

Putumayo

BRAZIL

PERU

Amazonas

N
W   E
S

Leticia

Geopolitical map
of Colombia

The Spaniards were soon dreaming up ways of draining the lake. In 1545, Gonzalo Jiménez de Quesada, the founder of Santafé de Bogotá, organized a bucket brigade of laborers with gourd containers. They reduced the level of the water by 9 feet (2.7 m). Next came Antonio de Sepúlveda, a wealthy merchant. He hired some 8,000 Indian workers to cut a large gap in the rim of the lake, allowing the water to drain. The level of the lake dropped another 65 feet (20 m), but the walls of the gap collapsed, killing many Indians, and the scheme was stopped.

In 1801, German scientist Alexander von Humboldt estimated how much gold there might be. He based his calculations on 1,000 pilgrims visiting the lake over a period of 100 years and arrived at a figure of $300 million. But Monsieur de la Kier of Paris, a French scholar, put the stakes much higher. He calculated a staggering total of more than 1 billion British pounds.

Then José Ignacio "Pepe" París tried to dig a trench that would allow the water to escape from the lake, but rocks and earth fell into the trench. He tried to shore up the sides, but that did not work, nor did a tunnel he started to dig 30 feet (9 m) below the lake.

The closest the lake ever came to revealing its secrets was at the beginning of this century when a company called Contractors Ltd. bought the rights to investigate. Using a 1,312-foot (400-m)-long tunnel and a system of sluice gates, the company managed to drain the lake, and took a photograph to prove it.

On the first day it was drained, the lake bed was so wet and slimy that no one could walk on it. By the next day, the sun had dried it out, but the mud was as hard as concrete. It took several weeks to get drilling equipment that would penetrate the surface, and by then it was too late. The mud had sealed the tunnel and blocked the sluice gates, and the lake had filled up again with the spring rains. Since 1965, Lake Guatavita has been protected as part of the country's national heritage. For now, the secrets of El Dorado are safe.

Today, Colombia has "new gold." It has been around even longer than the gold of Lake Guatavita, but it has only been exploited—and with devastating effects—within the past few decades. Sometimes called "green gold," the leafy coca plant grows mainly in the valleys and slopes of the Andes Mountains in Bolivia and Peru. Its leaves have been chewed, mixed with lime and ash, by native Andean peoples for hundreds of years. Coca plays an important part in their religious ceremonies. Modern-day travelers drink coca tea to help offset the effects of high altitude.

But coca is also the basis of the illegal drug cocaine. Although Colombia grows little of the plant, it is brought in from Peru and Bolivia and processed in Colombian factories. Many such factories are hidden in Colombia's jungles and forests. It is then shipped to the United States, Europe, and around the world through a variety of routes designed to avoid detection by drug agents and security officers.

Coca leaves drying in the sun

A canoe glides along the banks of a rain forest.

Colombia's drug trafficking is controlled by groups in Cali and Medellín, two of the country's largest cities. Enormous amounts of money change hands, and the constant rivalry between the drug-running groups has caused great upheaval in Colombia. Frequent bombings have occurred, especially between 1989 and 1991, and hundreds of assassinations. Even judges are in fear of their lives, and no one who attempts to bring the criminals to justice is safe. Penalties are never imposed for 95 percent of the cases taken to court. Some drug runners have been caught or killed, but despite considerable support from the U.S. Drug Enforcement Agency (DEA) and advice from experts worldwide, the illegal trade continues.

Colombia now has a tarnished image, which is sad for a country that has so much else to offer. Its landscapes are stunning, its economy is strong, there is a wealth of historical treasures, and the lives of some of its ethnic peoples have hardly changed in centuries.

Country of Contrasts

Colombia is the fourth-largest country in South America and the only one to have a coastline on both the Pacific Ocean and the Caribbean Sea. Between the two lies the Isthmus of Panama, a small neck of land that connects Colombia with Central America. To the east, Colombia shares borders with Venezuela and Brazil. Peru and Ecuador lie to the south.

Bahía Taganga is on Colombia's Caribbean coast.

Sierra Nevada de Santa Marta

N O OTHER COUNTRY IN THE WORLD OFFERS SUCH A contrast. In Colombia you can dive among the living corals of a tropical sea and glance up at snowclad mountains. The best spot to do this is a few miles east of Santa Marta, a historic town on the Caribbean coast.

The distance from the palm-fringed beaches to the snowy summit of Pico Cristóbal Colón, Colombia's highest mountain, is less than 35 miles (56 km). The mountain, which is named after Christopher Columbus, is 18,947 feet (5,775 m) high, just 1,373 feet (419 m) less than Alaska's Mount McKinley, the highest peak in North America.

Opposite: **Colombia's rain forests contain countless species of plants and animals.**

Historic Santa Marta, on the Caribbean coast

Pico Cristóbal Colón is Colombia's highest mountain.

Dirt tracks through the Guajira peninsula are sometimes impassable.

Cristóbal Colón is just one of several towering peaks in the Sierra Nevada de Santa Marta, a small and isolated mountain region overlooking the Caribbean Sea. The first explorers to cross the ocean from Spain saw the snows of the Sierra Nevada from many miles out at sea.

The Sierra Nevada mountains are roughly triangular, with the northern side facing the sea and the Guajira, a desert peninsula of scrub-covered land. This wilderness juts into the Caribbean and is shared with Venezuela, which owns a narrow strip on the southeastern side. The Guajira is Colombia's only large desert area.

The western side of the Sierra Nevada de Santa Marta has many small rivers that rush down the mountains to fill its swampy lowlands. This is a land of shallow lagoons and large mangrove swamps.

On the southeast, the Sierra Nevada overlook the Andes Mountains, the second-longest mountain chain in the world. The Andes stretch 4,500 miles (7,200 km) from Colombia to the southernmost tip of South America.

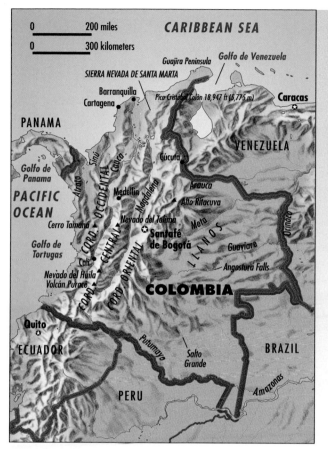

Geographical Features

Area: 439,735 square miles (1,138,826 sq km)

Largest City: Santafé de Bogotá, population 6,004,782 (1996 estimate)

Highest Elevation: Pico Cristóbal Cólon, 18,947 feet (5,775 m) above sea level

Lowest Elevation: Sea level along the coasts

Longest Navigable River: Magdalena River, 956 miles (1,538 km) long, navigable for more than 930 miles (1,496 km)

Highest Waterfall: Catarata de Candelas at 984 feet (300 m) on the Cusiana River

Lowest Average Temperature: 46°F (8°C) in January in Santafé de Bogotá

Highest Average Temperature: 92°F (33°C) in July in Cali

Heaviest Annual Rainfall: Chocó with 394 inches (1,001 cm), one of the world's wettest areas

Deadliest Volcano: The Ruiz Volcano erupted in November 1985 and killed 25,000 people in Armero

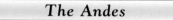

The Andes

The Andes Mountains in Colombia are divided into three *cordilleras* (mountain ranges). They fan out from the Ecuadorean border. To the east lies the Cordillera Oriental, the country's major mountain range. The Cordillera Central runs north to south through the middle of the country. To the west is the Cordillera Occidental, the lowest of the three ranges. The Magdalena River flows between the Oriental

A nineteenth-century mission in the Cordillera Central

A clock tower overlooks the village of Barichara, in Santander.

and Central, and the Cauca River flows between the Central and Occidental.

These Andean ranges are mostly covered with grasslands or the remains of forests. The higher altitudes, known as *páramos*, are still wild. Farmers in the valleys receive good rainfall.

Close to the border with Venezuela, the Cordillera Occidental descends steeply to the basin of Lake Maracaibo. Two departments in this region—Norte de Santander and Santander—are named after one of Colombia's national heroes.

Francisco de Paula Santander

Francisco de Paula Santander was born in April 1792 at a *hacienda* (large estate) near Villa del Rosario, which now lies close to Venezuela. Today, the town houses a small museum dedicated to its most famous son and the place where the first constitution of the Gran Colombia union of countries was signed. This was a success that Santander had helped to create.

Santander was initially a strong supporter of Simón Bolívar, who masterminded the movement for independence from Spain. From the age of twenty, Santander was at the center of the battles that led eventually to the removal of the Spaniards. By twenty-eight, he was vice president of Gran Colombia under Bolívar. Santander was a federalist and opposed central government for the countries of Gran Colombia, however. He was exiled in 1828. On Bolívar's death, Santander was recalled from exile and served as president from 1832 to 1836. He died in Santafé de Bogotá in 1840.

The Cordillera Oriental

The highest peak in the Cordillera Oriental is Alto Ritacuva at 18,021 feet (5,493 m). It rises in the Nevada de Cocuy, a cluster of snowy summits on the border with Venezuela. Southward from this point the mountains curve to the southwest and embrace the province of *Cundinamarca* (Land of the Condor), where the capital city of Santafé de Bogotá stands at 8,563 feet (2,610 m) on a level plain, or *sabana* (savanna).

Low ranges surround Santafé de Bogotá, and to the east their slopes descend abruptly through forests to vast areas of low-lying prairies known as the *llanos*. Rivers flow from the mountains

The Cordillera Oriental is Colombia's major mountain range.

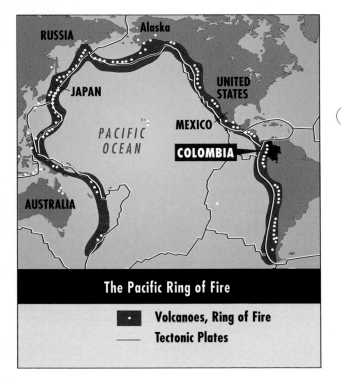

The Pacific Ring of Fire

• Volcanoes, Ring of Fire
— Tectonic Plates

The slopes of the Galeras Volcano rise behind the small city of Pasto.

across the llanos to the Orinoco River. To the south, other rivers flow eastward to the Amazon basin.

The Cordillera Central

The Andean range that sweeps from Colombia to the far south is young by geological standards—about 40 million years old. Earth's crust is made up of seven large pieces and many smaller ones, called plates, that fit together like the pieces of a jigsaw puzzle. The plates, which carry the continents and oceans, float on Earth's mantle—a layer of soft, molten rock below the crust. In some places, plates are pushed together. As they collide, land is pushed up to form mountains. The Andes Mountains are now rising slowly like a giant wrinkle on the face of the planet. Sometimes plate movements cause volcanoes to spew fire and lava and earthquakes to heave the ground.

In Colombia, the Cordillera Central is most active. The country's highest Andean peak, the Nevado del Huila at 18,865 feet (5,750 m), is an old volcano. Other volcanoes are better known because they have erupted in recent years. In the far south, the Galeras Volcano near the small city of Pasto

The Armero Disaster

Armero was a quiet little town where the people worked in cotton production and grew coffee. Potatoes were cultivated on the slopes of the Ruiz Volcano.

In November 1985, the volcano erupted, melting about 10 percent of its icy core. When the side of the volcano collapsed, a mudflow sent millions of tons of ice, slush, and volcanic debris on a deadly high-speed run that swept over Armero and a nearby village. Many people were asleep when the 15-foot (4.6-m)-high wave of mud buried their homes. Twenty-five thousand people died, making it one of the world's most lethal eruptions in the twentieth century. The children at right are among those orphaned by the disaster.

erupted in January 1993, killing nine research scientists. It also damaged crops and local homesteads.

Puracé Volcano towers 15,604 feet (4,756 m) over the historic town of Popayán. This is an area of great subterranean activity with hot springs and steaming vents on the surface. In March 1983, Popayán was struck by an earthquake that

Earthquake victims wait in line to receive aid in the historic town of Popayán.

caused hundreds of casualties. In January 1999, hundreds more died in an earthquake in Armenia. Most tragic was the disaster at Armero in the shadow of the Nevado del Ruiz (Ruiz Volcano).

The Chocó

The Cordillera Occidental lies between the center of Colombia and the Pacific Ocean. This range is lower than the other two, with a high point of 13,780 feet (4,200 m) at Cerro Tamaná. A narrow strip of low-level land separates the foothills from the sea. The only elevation on the coast is the narrow Serrania de Baudó, with its highest point the Alto de Buey at 5,939 feet (1,810 meters).

The Chocó is the region close to the Pacific. It stretches from the swamps of the Darién in the north southward for about 550 miles (885 km). The Chocó is one of the world's wettest places.

Transporting plantains on the Atrato River

The World's Wettest Place

The capital of the Chocó is Quibdó, a city of about 60,000 people that lies at approximately the same longitude as Washington, D.C. Rainfall in Quibdó averages 324 inches (823 cm) annually, and in the record year of 1939 it reached more than 585 inches (1,500 cm).

Although the rainfall varies from north to south, the Chocó is probably the largest very wet region on earth. The land is mostly flat in the north with some hills in the south. The heavy rain creates spectacular rivers that crash through the canyons in a series of waterfalls and rapids. These rivers carry enormous quantities of water. The San Juan and the Atrato, which almost meet near Quibdó, were once used as a route between the Caribbean and Pacific. The San Juan flows to the west and the Atrato flows to the east. The Quibdó river market (right) is on the Atrato.

In some places there are large lagoons, and the coastline is fringed with swamps and mangrove forests. The dense rain forests that cover the lower levels of the Chocó are home to countless species of animals and plants. Many of the plants are world-record holders. One semi-parasitic plant has leaves more than 39 inches (1 m) long and 19 inches (.5 m) wide.

The River Valleys

The Magdalena River, the largest river in Colombia, rises in the far south of the Cordillera Central on an upland known as Páramo del Buey. The river then flows north 956 miles (1,538 km) to the Caribbean and its mouth near the port of Barranquilla, west of the Sierra Nevada de Santa Marta. The Magdalena empties into the sea by a main channel and a maze of waterways where large lagoons have formed.

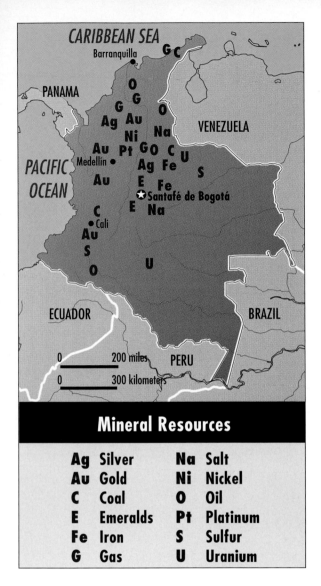

Mineral Resources

Ag	Silver	Na	Salt
Au	Gold	Ni	Nickel
C	Coal	O	Oil
E	Emeralds	Pt	Platinum
Fe	Iron	S	Sulfur
G	Gas	U	Uranium

The Cauca River rises on the western side of the Páramo del Buey and flows 838 miles (1,348 km) northward through rich land. Cali, the main city of the Cauca valley, is a flourishing industrial center. Eventually the Cauca joins the Magdalena in flatlands about 120 miles (193 km) from the sea. The lower course of the Magdalena is wide and shallow and was plied by paddle steamers (old Mississippi–style steamboats) until the 1960s.

The Llanos

The llanos are vast grasslands that lie to the east of the Andes. Together with the Amazon region, they cover more than two-thirds of Colombia. The llanos extend into the Orinoco region of Venezuela, creating the largest savanna in South America.

The llanos are exceptionally flat lands. They were formed about 60 million years ago by sediments carried into a vast natural basin from surrounding mountains that were beginning to rise. As the basin filled, the rivers carved their way across its plains. Even now, these rivers carry sediments to the Orinoco River and onward to the delta at its mouth in Venezuela.

Villavicencio (population 252,711), at the foot of the Cordillera Oriental, is considered the capital of the llanos region. It is only 69 miles (111 km) from Santafé de Bogotá

Looking at Colombian Cities

Cali (below), Colombia's second-largest city, was founded in 1536 by Sebastián de Belalcázar. Today, the city is southwestern Colombia's center of industry (paper and chemicals), farming, and trade. It's also known for salsa music. Cali residents take pride in the Pan-American Sports Complex and La Plaza de Toros de Cañaveralejo, the country's largest bullring. Recently, Cali has become known as the world capital of the cocaine drug trade. The

year-round average temperature in Cali is 75°F (24°C) although summer temperatures are often above 90°F (32°C).

Medellín (right), a busy manufacturer of food products and textiles in the Central Cordillera, was founded in 1616 by Jewish settlers from Spain. The city is also a major coffee market. Medellín has many museums, including the Museum of Modern Art and the Museum of Anthropology. Medellín is called the City of Eternal Spring because it enjoys an average year-round temperature of 71°F (22°C).

Barranquilla, founded in 1629, is Colombia's main seaport and a center of industry (textiles) and trade on the Caribbean. Hot, wet weather with an average year-round temperature of 82°F (28°C) often makes life uncomfortable in Barranquilla. Thousands of the city's residents and visitors enjoy four days of Carnaval each year before Ash Wednesday and the beginning of Lent.

Cartagena, founded in 1533 by Pedro de Heredia, is Colombia's second-largest port. This beautiful Caribbean city is rich in history. Walls built to protect the city from pirates in the 1500s and 1700s still stand. Churches and homes from those years are still in use. Many of the homes are museums today. Cartagena's climate is similar to Barranquilla's.

over a spectacular mountain road, but it is almost at the end of the asphalt highway. The road continues for about 50 miles (80 km) and then grasslands stretch to the horizon. There are unpaved tracks through the grasslands, but many are impassable in the wet season.

Colombia's Amazon

Colombia's Amazon region south of the llanos is part of the enormous Amazon River basin. The Amazon River flows from its source in the Peruvian Andes in a generally west-to-east direction near the equator. A small part of Colombia lies along the north bank of the Amazon almost 2,000 miles (3,200 km) from its mouth at the Atlantic Ocean.

The principal Colombian town and port in that area is Leticia, with a population of 32,700. It is connected with the rest of the country only by air or by a very uncomfortable boat and bus journey. Only 50 miles (80 km) of Colombia's land lies along the Amazon River, but dozens of its tributaries begin in Colombia's mountains.

One of these, the Putumayo River, begins near the mountain town of Pasto. It tumbles down the Andes through dense forests to the lowlands, where it forms Colombia's border with Ecuador and Peru.

Boats are an important means of transportation in the Amazon port of Leticia.

The Islands

Colombia also has several small islands. The largest are San Andrés and Providencia, which lie in the Caribbean Sea about 480 miles (772 km) northwest of Barranquilla near Nicaragua.

Several more small islands are nearer the Colombian mainland. The most frequently visited are the Islas del Rosario, close to the coast near Cartagena, a historic fortified city on the Caribbean coast.

The Pacific coast has a few small islands, most of which are near the shore. The most famous is Gorgona Island, about 18 miles (30 km) off the coast, which was once used as a prison. Today it is a national park and a scuba divers' paradise. Another island, Malpelo, less than 1 mile (1.6 km) long, lies 300 miles (480 km) out to sea off Buenaventura.

Gorgona Island, off the Pacific coast, was once used as a prison.

THREE

A Naturalist's El Dorado

Colombia holds several world records. It is second only to Brazil in its number of known plant species, and it has 1,754 species of birds—more than any other country and almost 20 percent of the world's total. Brazil has about 18 percent of the world's bird species and Africa has 15 percent.

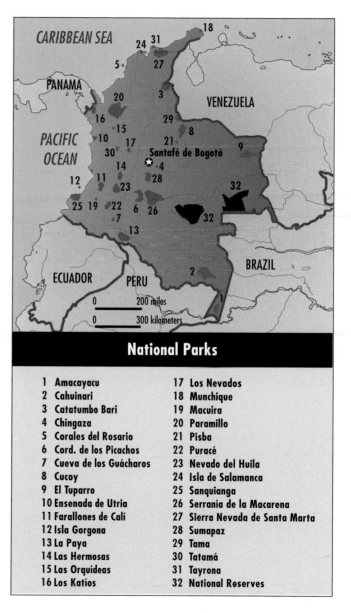

OLOMBIA IS ALSO FIRST IN THE number of orchid and palm species, second in amphibians, and third in reptiles. Even more remarkable, 10 percent of the world's species live in Colombia although it covers less than 1 percent of the world's territory.

The country's great biodiversity is largely due to its incredible variety of habitats. Colombia's many kinds of forests range from scrub forest to rain forest. It has deserts, swamps, seas, lakes, and rivers as well as many more specialized habitats.

Sierra Nevada de Santa Marta

The Sierra Nevada de Santa Marta and the nearby lagoons are an example of Colombia's diversity. Each side of the Sierra Nevada has a different climate, and the vegetation changes at each level. Where the rainfall is

National Parks

1	Amacayacu	17	Los Nevados
2	Cahuinari	18	Munchique
3	Catatumbo Bari	19	Macuira
4	Chingaza	20	Paramillo
5	Corales del Rosario	21	Pisba
6	Cord. de los Picachos	22	Puracé
7	Cueva de los Guácharos	23	Nevado del Huila
8	Cucoy	24	Isla de Salamanca
9	El Tuparro	25	Sanquianga
10	Ensenada de Utria	26	Serranía de la Macarena
11	Farallones de Cali	27	Sierra Nevada de Santa Marta
12	Isla Gorgona	28	Sumapaz
13	La Paya	29	Tama
14	Las Hermosas	30	Tatamá
15	Las Orquideas	31	Tayrona
16	Los Katios	32	National Reserves

heavy, the forests are thick with tangled vines, tree ferns, and moss-covered trees. These forests often are bathed in mist. Here the brilliantly colored birds include the trogons. The spectacular quetzal, which lives in Central America, is a trogon.

Bromeliads, often kept as houseplants, grow on the trees. Many have deep clusters of leaves where rainwater collects. These natural "tanks" provide a home for insect larvae and even for tiny frogs.

The north and east sides of the Sierra Nevada are dry at the lower levels. Spiny trees have small leaves that reduce water loss. Iguana lizards up to 39 inches (1 m) long live here, along with shoelace-thin snakes whose colors blend with the yellowing vines, and huge tortoises. Other unusual animals

Trogons have brightly colored plumage.

Opposite: **Bromeliads grow on trees in the rain forest.**

Iguanas thrive in dry regions.

This anteater is hunting for insects to eat.

include anteaters, sloths, and armadillos. These very different animals are all closely related. Their common ancestor lived in Central and South America about 65 million years ago.

Tayrona Turtles

Many Tayrona beaches are nesting sites for female green turtles. They come out of the sea at night to lay their eggs above the high-water mark, often among the first line of coconut palms. The turtles scoop out nests in the sand and lay thousands of eggs. Each turtle lays about 100 eggs up to four times during a nesting season.

When the young turtles hatch, they have to make their own way back across the beach to the sea. They run a grisly gauntlet of predators. On land, small carnivores such as coatis, which are related to racoons, as well as opossums and small wild members of the cat family prey on the baby turtles. Dogs kept by villagers are another danger, as are numerous birds of prey. It is amazing that any of these young turtles survive.

National Parks

Sadly, the Sierra Nevada is no longer in a pristine natural condition. For many years, the area has been subjected to logging and settlement, especially at levels where coffee grows well. And hunters have affected every form of wildlife. To try to control the threats to the area, the Colombian government has established two national parks here.

One of these, Tayrona National Park, lies mostly at a low level. It includes wide beaches where turtles nest, and nearby coral reefs. The other, the Sierra Nevada de Santa Marta National Park, covers the unique mountain forest zone all the way up to the snow line.

These parks are part of a national system of fifty-six protected areas that cover the nation's immense variety of natural life. A special office of the Ministry of the Environment is responsible for these protected areas.

In the Mountains

Except for a few isolated places, the Andean ranges are heavily cultivated and the forests are logged. However, some areas have been set aside as reserves. El Cocuy and Tama in the Cordillera Oriental are two reserves where streams tumble from the heights through rock-filled valleys lined with tiny ferns and fungi. Higher up are alpine valleys carpeted with grassy slopes and brilliant with flowers. At the highest levels are *páramos* where the plants have adapted to survive extremes of cold and intense ultraviolet radiation from the sun.

Throughout the high mountain areas of Colombia and neighboring countries, the *páramos* have a landscape of their own. Often they are dotted with small lakes, pools, and boggy areas that are mist-shrouded for much of the year. A journey by foot across a *páramo* can be dangerous. Deep gullies are formed where water is constantly draining from the surface.

Among the most striking plants are the *frailejones* ("tall friars"). Related to the daisy, some species grow up to 10 to 12 feet (3 to 3.6 m) high. Like many other *páramo* plants, the *frailejones* have downy leaves to protect against the damp cold and the intense solar radiation.

Animal life is not as immediately obvious in the highlands, though there are numerous species of birds including several tiny hummingbirds. Some birds are seen even at the snow line. Among the special animals of the *páramos* are frogs that carry their eggs on their back; worms almost 5 feet

The National Tree: The Wax Palm

The scientific name of this elegant tree—*Ceroxylon quindiensis*—tells most of the story. The name comes from two Greek words—*keros*, meaning "wax," and *xylon*, meaning "wood." *Quindiensis* means that the species was first known in Quindío, a department in the Cordillera Central.

But the name does not tell us the bad news. The national tree has been in danger for some time as more forestland is cut down for farms. The seedlings do not do well in sunlight, and they are often eaten by grazing cattle. Another threat comes from a previously unknown disease that has affected more than half the trees in some areas. Scientists are working to find a remedy.

The harsh landscape of the Desert of Tatacoa

(1.5 m) long; and a rare mountain tapir—a mammal related to the horse and the rhinoceros.

Not all of the Colombian Andes are forested. In some areas, the land is very dry, even desertlike. The Desert of Tatacoa, in the upper valley of the Magdalena River, has a desolate, eroded landscape covered with cacti and scrubland plants. The land has been further damaged by goats overgrazing. Oddly enough, this barren area is surrounded by green mountain vegetation.

The slopes of the higher volcanoes are covered with mosses and lichens. Puracé Volcano National Park has hot springs, rivers flowing with sulfurous, milky water, and waterfalls. Condors, which were on the verge of extinction in Colombia, are found in this remote area. A program for reintroduction of young condors raised in captivity is progressing well with the help of zoos in the United States.

Among the mammals of these damp Andean forests are the mountain paca—a rodent as big as a small dog—and the only South American bear. It is called the "spectacled bear," for the markings around its eyes.

In the Grasslands

East of the Cordillera Oriental, the llanos stretch to the ancient mountains of Venezuela. Rivers crisscross the grasslands and flood huge areas every rainy season. After the rains, pools of water remain for months. Here many species of water birds gather, sometimes in enormous numbers. Tree-ducks form large colonies, as do thousands of herons. The rivers and pools are

A Noanoma flute player with his pet paca

Oilbirds

Oilbirds get their name from the days when Native Americans collected these young birds from their nests to get large quantities of oil for cooking. The birds feed on the oily fruit of palms, and young nestlings quickly become half as heavy again as their parents. Oilbirds nest on ledges in caves and feed at night. Like bats, they find their way around the caves by echolocation—they make a strange clicking sound as they fly. They also have a shrieking call that is deafening in a cave with hundreds of birds milling around.

The largest oilbird colony in Colombia is in the *Cueva de los Guácharos* (Cave of the Oilbirds) in the Cordillera Oriental. This cave, which is in a national park, is home to approximately 2,000 birds. The cave floor, littered with the remains of palm fruit, provides yet another special habitat. It is literally crawling with cave-dwelling invertebrates such as spiders, isopods, and beetles.

La Macarena

In southeast Columbia, an area of outstanding biological value is threatened. The *Serranía de la Macarena*, a small, isolated range of flat-topped mountains, rises close to the Cordillera Oriental. The richness of the area's flora and fauna has been recognized for a long time, and the Macarena was declared a conservation area in 1948. The reason for the great variety of species is the area's isolation and its unique location at the meeting of three distinct natural areas—the Andes Mountains and the Orinoco and Amazon Rivers.

Human activity in the Macarena was once almost nonexistent, but in recent years loggers, farmers, hunters, and prospectors have moved in. The area is now endangered, and the only safe future for wildlife lies in a national park that has been established on the eastern side of the range.

Some of the mammals there are very rare, such as the giant otter, a 7-foot (2-m) -long carnivore (above), and some of the caimans. Also under threat are the many edible species such as the deer, the giant armadillo, and floor-dwelling rodents such as agoutis, pacas, and pacaranas that are killed for their meat.

home to South American crocodilians—the caimans—but their numbers have been reduced by hunters. Of the mammals, the largest rodent, the semiaquatic capybara, lives near pools and rivers, coming to the grasslands to browse.

Colombia's Amazon has all the variety of this enormous natural resource. The rain forests in Colombia, like those in other countries, have been cut back at a steady rate since the 1960s, especially along the edges of the Andean cordilleras. In these regions, trees grow up to 150 feet (45.7 m) and the forest canopy is filled with wildlife. Birds and butterflies and other insects abound. Spider monkeys, howler monkeys, and capuchins are still found in many areas. The tinier primates, such as marmosets and tamarins, are also plentiful.

The rivers are flanked with lagoons, which are often covered with giant water lilies—the gorgeous *Victoria regia*. These lagoons are havens for many water birds, including herons, egrets, and storks. Caimans are rare but in some places they are gradually returning. The rivers are home to many species of fish, including large catfish that can weigh more than 200 pounds (91 kg).

Chocó Frogs

Long ago, the Native American people of the Chocó forests realized that a tiny, very colorful frog they called *kōkoé* was highly poisonous. Its colors probably evolved as a warning to other animals—a "keep off" signal. These tiny frogs belong to a group known as the poison-arrow, or poison-dart, frogs. They are found throughout many of the wetter tropical forests of northern South America and Central America. The Chocó Indians discovered that the skin of the frogs contains a powerful poison, which they could use on the tips of their blowgun darts for hunting. Researchers have since learned that the poison is one of the most deadly known to science.

A Rich History

Sometime during the last Ice Age about 10,000 to 15,000 years ago, people migrated over the frozen Bering Strait from Asia into America. Gradually making their way south, they crossed the narrow Isthmus of Panama and reached Colombia, the gateway to South America. Some settled along the way; others continued to the far south of the continent. In Colombia they settled in small areas of the Andes Mountains and on the Pacific and Caribbean coasts.

O VER THE CENTURIES THE NEWCOMERS survived by hunting, fishing, and gathering nuts and seeds from the forests. About 3,000 to 4,000 years ago, people in the Andes began to grow corn and other crops. They then were able to settle in one area and develop organized societies.

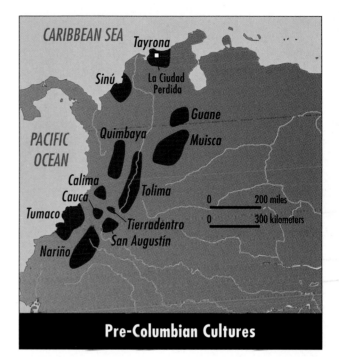

Pre-Columbian Cultures

In Colombia, the Muisca, also known as the Chibcha, became the most important of these peoples. They lived on the large plain around present-day Santafé de Bogotá. The Tayrona lived in highlands to the north near the Caribbean coast, and the Sinú settled in the lower Magdalena valley. Most of the other peoples, including the Quimbaya, Tolima, Calima, Nariño, San Agustín, and Tierradentro, lived in the central and southern highlands. The Tumaco settled on the Pacific coast.

When the Spaniards arrived early in the sixteenth century, the Muisca made up about one-third of Colombia's native population. They lived in thatched wooden huts in towns and villages.

Opposite: **Early civilizations in Colombia created beautiful gold objects.**

The Muisca farmed the fertile land, growing corn, potatoes, and a nutritious native cereal called *quinoa*. They turned the land using simple wooden digging sticks and spades. They knew how to build agricultural terraces by cutting into the mountain slopes. Water flowed down the slopes of the terraces, making irrigation easier. Also, a variety of crops could be grown at different levels. Potatoes, for example, grow well in the cooler, higher climate, while maize and fruit grow better on lower levels. The Muisca's only domesticated animals were dogs and guinea pigs.

Although other cultures lived in a similar way to the Muiscas, there were some differences. The Sinú preferred large huts where many families lived together, while others, such as the Quimbaya, lived in separate communities with small populations. Almost all these groups worshiped the sun, moon, and other natural forces as gods and made offerings to them. Generally, the people wore simple clothing, such as cotton tunics or breeches and shirts. The Muiscas wore ear or nose plugs.

Statues of San Agustín

Colombia's most famous archaeological site is San Agustín, near Popayán. It is a hilly region covered with more than 500 carved stone figures and several tombs. Pottery and gold have been found in some of the tombs.

Many of the statues represent gods that are part human and part animal. Some have big, round eyes, while the eyes of others are long, narrow slits. Other statues depict sacred animals such as the eagle, a symbol of power and light, and the frog, which is associated with water. Others show a jaguar or a catlike figure with large fangs.

Not far from San Agustín is Tierradentro, a site with about 100 underground burial chambers carved out of rock. Spiral staircases built into the rock lead to some of the burial vaults. Several vaults have domelike ceilings supported by huge rock pillars.

Most of the Native American cultures were skilled potters and excellent goldsmiths. Much of the gold came from riverbeds, though some was extracted from deep shafts in the mountains. Where there was no gold, the Indians traded fish, salt, and cloth for the precious metal.

Opposite: **The Muisca were farming quinoa cereal when Spanish explorers arrived in Colombia.**

A Rich History **43**

The Lost City

The Tayrona of the Sierra Nevada mountains were among the most advanced of the early civilizations. Their engineers built stone roads, reservoirs, and bridges over a wide area. Archaeologists have found small settlements of a few houses and large towns with 1,000 or more dwellings. In 1975, the discovery of *La Ciudad Perdida* (The Lost City) further confirmed the Tayronas' skills as builders and artisans.

Ceremonial sites at the Lost City of the Tayrona

The wood-and-thatch houses have disappeared, but it is possible to see from the foundations that the dwellings were divided into separate sections for men and women. In the women's area, utensils such as pots, water jars, and grinding stones were found, while the men's area contained stone axes and chisels, weights for fishing nets, and fine pottery. The ceremonial houses were much larger than the dwellings, with causeways and stairways. Stone jars that held ritual objects were buried under stone slabs with many pieces of goldwork.

The Spaniards Arrive

Serious attempts to settle Colombia's Caribbean coast did not begin until several years after Christopher Columbus arrived in the New World in 1492. Colombia's oldest town, Santa Marta, was founded in 1525. Cartagena was founded in 1533. Expeditions to open up the interior were driven by the Spaniards' obsession with gold. The first expedition set off from the coast in 1536.

Gonzalo Jiménez de Quesada Expedition

The leader of the 1536 expedition, Gonzalo Jiménez de Quesada, was probably aiming to reach the kingdom of the Incas in Peru, whose reputation for wealth and gold

Gonzalo Jiménez de Quesada

was widespread. Jiménez de Quesada pushed up the Magdalena River through swamps infested with alligators and snakes.

He encountered hostile Indians and his soldiers were starving, but somewhere along the route, perhaps having heard of rich salt mines, emeralds, and the legend of El Dorado, he abandoned the river. Jiménez de Quesada then climbed the Cordillera Oriental and arrived in the land of the Muiscas.

At that time, the Muiscas were divided into clans headed by the Zipa and the Zaque, who were at war with each other. The weakness of their situation helped Jiménez de Quesada to conquer the territory without much difficulty. He looted the royal capital of the Zaque, taking 150,000 pesos of gold and 230 emeralds. He founded Santafé de Bogotá in 1538.

Nicolaus Federmann Expedition

Meanwhile, another expedition was approaching Muisca territory from the east, led by Nicolaus Federmann, a German. In 1537, Federmann headed out of Venezuela across the vast grasslands toward the Andes. Within forty days he climbed from near sea level to a height of over 11,500 feet (3,500 m). It was intensely cold, and more than two-thirds of his men died on the way. Eventually he reached Muisca territory, only to find that Jiménez de Quesada had arrived there first.

Sebastián de Belalcázar Expedition

Sebastián de Belalcázar served in Peru with Francisco Pizarro during the conquest of the Incas. After receiving his share of the Inca treasure, he advanced north to Ecuador. There the

A street in the town of
Popayán today

story goes, he heard of "a certain king who went naked aboard a raft...powdered gold from head to foot," and he decided to push on. On his way he founded the towns of Pasto and Popayán in southern Colombia. In the Magdalena River valley he also encountered the fierce Panches and Pijaos in the land of the Tolima. These fearsome warrior tribes were cannibals and strongly resisted the Europeans.

When the leaders of the three expeditions finally, and unexpectedly, met up in the land of the Muisca, they did not fight one another. Instead, they came to an agreement that led to the creation of the *audiencia* of Santafé de Bogotá by the Spanish crown in 1549. The *audiencia* was a kind of council that managed the affairs of the conquered territory. It was controlled by the Viceroyalty of Peru, based in Lima. In effect, the conquered area was now a colony of Spain.

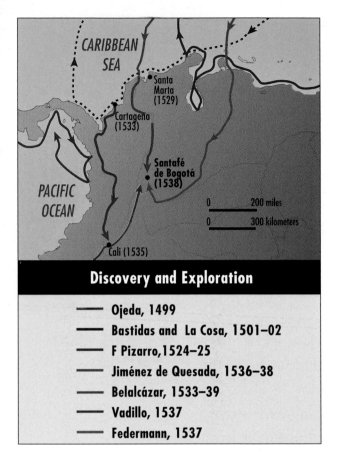

CARIBBEAN
SEA

Santa
Marta
(1529)

Cartagena
(1533)

PACIFIC
OCEAN

Santafé
de Bogotá
(1538)

0   200 miles
0   300 kilometers

Cali (1535)

Discovery and Exploration

—— Ojeda, 1499
—— Bastidas and La Cosa, 1501–02
—— F Pizarro,1524–25
—— Jiménez de Quesada, 1536–38
—— Belalcázar, 1533–39
—— Vadillo, 1537
—— Federmann, 1537

Life in the Colony

The economy of the colony was based on mining—mainly gold, emeralds, and salt—and on farming. The land was rich and fertile and the Spaniards forced the Native Americans to work it. The natives were treated like slaves. They were forced to work for the Spanish settlers and pay a tribute, or tax, to the Spanish crown.

Native Americans who worked in the mines were treated as brutally as those who worked on the land. Many died of diseases brought by the Europeans, such as smallpox and influenza. Those least affected lived in remote parts of the llanos grasslands and Amazon forests.

Starting in the sixteenth century, black African slaves were imported to work on the sugar plantations and in the mines. Gradually, the racial mix of the population began to change. *Mestizos* were people of Spanish and Native American parentage, *mulatos* were of Spanish and African unions, and *zambos* were a mix of African and Native American peoples. The Spaniards kept all the power throughout the colonial period. Spaniards born in Spain were known as *peninsulares*, while Spaniards born in the colony were called *criollos*.

Cartagena and the Pirates

Cartagena became one of Spain's principal Caribbean ports. Gold, silver, and other treasures from the countries of South America were sent across the Isthmus of Panama to Cartagena for shipment to Europe. A heavily guarded convoy set out once a year, and the city became the focus of continued attacks from pirates.

The French pirates Jean and Martin Côte raided Cartagena in 1560, and in 1586 Sir Francis Drake inflicted heavy damage. With 1,300 men, he captured the city, looted it for a month, burned down some 200 houses, and destroyed the half-finished cathedral. Then he made off with 107,000 gold ducats.

An early map of Cartagena, from an account of Sir Francis Drake's voyage

Sir Francis Drake

Cartagena

Cartagena today has many reminders of its history. The thick walls still stand around the city with a yellow clocktower above the main entrance. The nearby *Plaza de los Coches* (Square of the Carriages) was once a bustling slave market where arrivals from Africa were sold to new masters. Not far away is the Cathedral of San Pedro Claver, named after the priest who devoted his life to caring for the slaves.

Near the cathedral is the Palace of the Inquisition, a notorious place where the Spaniards used dreadful punishment to subdue people of other religious faiths. Fine old mansions and houses with balconies and colonial arches line most of the streets.

Outside the city walls stands the great fort of San Felipe with battlements, underground tunnels, terraces, and guardhouses. A statue of Blas de Lezo guards the fort. Beyond San Felipe is La Popa hill, crowned by the convent of *Nuestra Señora de la Candelaria* (Our Lady of the Candlemas), known as the "Patron Saint of Pirate Attacks." From La Popa there is a magnificent view of the city below.

The people of Cartagena countered by building a series of forts and encircling the town with a wall 39 feet (12 m) high and 56 feet (17 m) thick, with six gates. Nevertheless, the French admiral Baron de Pointis, with 10,000 men, beat down the defenses in 1697 and ravaged the city. Then, in 1741, Sir Edward Vernon, a British admiral with 27,000 troops and 186 warships, besieged the city for six weeks. Anticipating victory, Sir Edward sent word to England that the attack was successful. It was not. The Cartagenians, led by the one-eyed, one-legged, one-armed Blas de Lezo, fought off the attack and captured some 2,000 British troops.

Independence

In 1717, the Spanish crown created the Viceroyalty of New Granada with Santafé de Bogotá as its capital. The Viceroyalty was made of what are now the countries of Colombia, Panama, Venezuela, and Ecuador. During the eighteenth century, people in the colonies grew increasingly unhappy with Spanish rule. They objected to paying taxes to the Spanish crown and to Spain's control of their trade. The colonies were not allowed to trade with any country other than Spain. This was particularly resented by the criollos. Criollos were greatly involved in trade because they were excluded from most senior posts in government by the peninsulares. In Colombia, however, the criollos had the support of the church and some wealthy landowners.

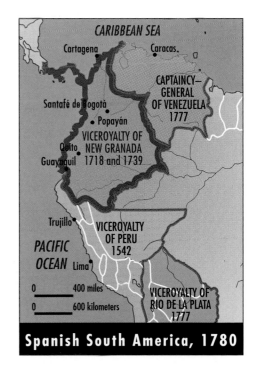

Spanish South America, 1780

The first open rebellion against the Spanish crown took place in 1781, but it was brutally crushed. However, the colonists' spirit was rekindled when Antonio Nariño translated Thomas Paine's *Rights of Man* in 1794. In this work, Paine defended the French Revolution and encouraged the English to overthrow their monarchy and form a republic.

Events in Europe precipitated the movement to independence. In 1808, French emperor Napoleon Bonaparte removed the Spanish king from his throne and proclaimed his own son Joseph Bonaparte king of Spain. The colony saw its chance to reject the Spanish monarchy. But while most people agreed on separation from Spain, they did not agree on how the colony should be run. The Centralists wanted government from Santafé de Bogotá, while the Federalists wanted more power for the provinces. The result of this disagreement was civil war.

When the Spanish king regained his throne in 1814, the civil war in Colombia made it easier for his forces to regain control there. However, in the reign of terror that followed, hundreds of people were executed and the countryside was ravaged. The colonists became even more determined to gain independence.

Federalist troops escaped into the llanos and regrouped under General Francisco de Paula Santander. They joined forces with Simón Bolívar. Bolívar had achieved great success in Venezuela, followed by defeat and exile. On returning to Venezuela, he assembled an army of fearless and tough horsemen from the llanos.

In May 1819, Bolívar started his famous march from the flooded Venezuelan plains across the cold, windswept cordilleras to the savanna of Santafé de Bogotá. There, on August 7, 1819, he defeated the Spanish forces at the Battle of Boyacá, and Colombia became independent.

Gran Colombia

Disagreement between the Centralists supported by Bolívar and the Federalists led by Santander continued even after the victory. Bolívar won, and in 1821 the new state of Gran Colombia was created with Bolívar as president and Santander as vice president. The new state was made up of Venezuela, Colombia, Panama (which was then part of Colombia), and Ecuador.

Simón Bolívar

Bolívar left almost immediately to help Peru gain its independence. It soon became clear that government of such a vast area was next to impossible. The Gran Colombia split up in 1830, and Bolívar died a lonely, disillusioned man that same year. Colombia became the Republic of the New Granada. It took back the name Colombia in 1863.

Rafael Núñez

Poet, philosopher, intellectual, and author of the national anthem, Rafael Núñez became president of Colombia in 1880. Though he was officially a Liberal, he held Conservative views and angered the Liberals by making Catholicism the state religion. In 1886, he produced the Constitution that remained in force until 1991. Núñez ruled like a dictator for three terms, ending in 1888. He opened the gates to Conservative rule for the next 42 years and was regarded as a traitor by many Liberals. He died in 1894.

Conservatives and Liberals

The Centralists and the Federalists became known as the Conservatives and the Liberals respectively. The wealthy and powerful Roman Catholic Church supported the Conservatives. The Liberals wanted to reduce the church's power. They also called for social reforms that included abolishing slavery and helping the poor.

The Conservatives agreed with some of the reforms, but for most of the nineteenth century Colombia was the scene of violent conflict and rebellions as the two sides squabbled. In 1899, a Liberal revolt turned into the War of a Thousand Days, which lasted until 1903. It was a full-scale civil war in which almost 100,000 people died, out of a population of only 4 million.

Panama's Independence

By the start of the 1900s, Panama was ready for independence from Colombia. Panama had become an important territory because its narrow isthmus was the shortest link between the Atlantic and Pacific Oceans. A canal at that point would

The Rubber Boom

At the beginning of this century, Colombia had border disputes with three of its neighbors— Venezuela, Ecuador, and Peru. The dispute with Peru was the most serious.

During the 1800s, rubber had become a valuable commodity. The process of vulcanization, which gave rubber elasticity and strength, made it especially suitable for the rainproof garments and Wellington boots fashionable at the time. With the arrival of the bicycle—and then the automobile— rubber was in huge demand for tires.

The best rubber came from the Amazon forests, where Native Americans were ruthlessly and cruelly forced to collect the latex sap from the trees. Some tribes were almost wiped out, while business owners made great fortunes. Colombia and Peru argued over an area around the River Putumayo where some of the best rubber trees were located. The dispute lasted for years, but eventually Colombia retained Leticia, its Amazon city.

spare ships from making the long journey around the distant south coast of South America.

The first attempt to build a canal, by France's Ferdinand de Lesseps, who had constructed the Suez Canal, failed. But the United States was interested and was also prepared to support Panama in its fight for independence. In return for its support, the United States was given the right to construct the Panama Canal and to control the land area known as the Panama Canal Zone.

Panama became independent in 1903, and the first ship passed through the Panama Canal in 1914. Colombia did not accept the situation until 1921, when the United States softened the blow with $25 million.

The Twentieth Century

The Conservatives remained in power in Colombia until 1930. It was a prosperous period, as the coffee and banana industries were developed and oil was discovered. But virtually nothing was done for the poor. When the Liberals returned to power, the poor were their first priority.

Liberal president Alfonso López Pumarejo instituted the Revolution on the March in the 1930s, paying particular attention to educational and medical needs of the poor. He also laid the groundwork for land reform that eventually took place in the 1960s.

When it came time for elections in 1946, the Liberal Party was so split that it ran two candidates, one moderate and one left-wing. The left-wing candidate was Jorge Eliecer Gaitán, a

"man of the people." Huge crowds of rural and urban poor attended his meetings and listened to his speeches.

Gaitán was assasinated in 1948 by Juan Roa Sierra. No one knows why because he was killed soon after by angry supporters of Gaitán. Gaitán's assassination unleashed an explosion of

A plaque marks the spot where Jorge Eliecer Gaitán was assassinated.

Crown of the Andes

In the late sixteenth century, the people of Popayán escaped a great smallpox epidemic that raged for three years in southern Colombia. They believed the Virgin Mother, patron of their cathedral, had protected them. In gratitude, they made her the most beautiful crown in the world. Inset with some 450 emeralds, it took twenty-four goldsmiths six years to make it.

The crown was placed on the statue of the Virgin Mother in December 1599. Over the years, more magnificent jewels and gold were added to it. More than once the Virgin Mother came close to losing her crown, as the cathedral was attacked by pirates, privateers, thieves, and revolutionaries.

In 1909, Popayán fell on hard times and wanted to sell the crown and use the money to build a much-needed orphanage, a hospital, and a home for the aged. The Vatican gave its permission, and in 1936 the crown was bought by an American group. No one really knew the value of the crown, but one estimate was 1.5 million British pounds (worth about U.S.$6 million at that time).

In 1995 the crown was up for sale again. It was auctioned in Sotheby's in London and Christie's in New York City, but no one bought it.

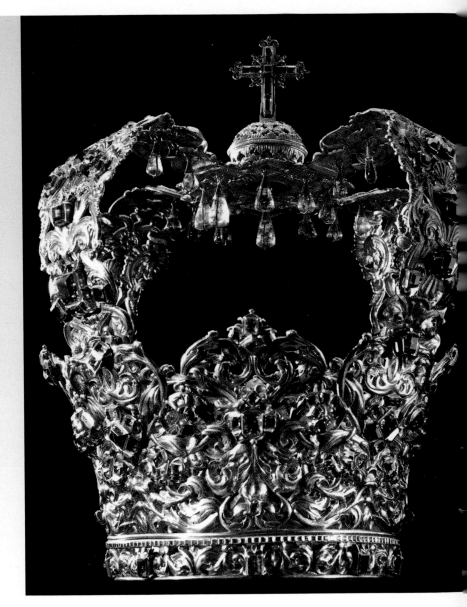

unprecedented violence in Colombia. First the capital was looted and many buildings were damaged or destroyed. Then the violence spread to the countryside. *La Violencia,* as it became known, lasted from 1948 to 1953 and erupted again from 1954 to 1962. It was an undeclared civil war in which more than 300,000 people died.

In 1958, the two parties created the National Front. The Liberals and Conservatives agreed that, until 1974, they would take turns holding power for four-year periods. Congress and all government and cabinet posts would be equally split between the two parties.

The first National Front president was a Liberal—Alberto Lleras Camargo, an internationally respected politician and diplomat. He was followed in 1962 by a Conservative, Guillermo León Valencia, who in turn was followed by a Liberal—Carlos Lleras Restrepo.

The National Front ended in 1974 when Conservative president Misael Pastrana Borrero completed his term. It had brought peace and some economic improvement. During these years, Colombia moved from a semi-feudal agricultural economy to a capitalist industrial state.

Governing the Republic

The National Front ended in 1974 with the election of Liberal president Alfonso López Michelsen. However, the arrangement to share power with the losing party lasted until 1986. In that year Liberal president Virgilio Barco Vargas formed a single-party administration.

WHEN THE LIBERAL César Gaviria Trujillo was elected president in 1990, he wanted to modernize the political system. The country was on the brink of chaos as a result of guerrilla activities and drug trafficking, and in a 1990 referendum the Colombian people voted for a Constitutional Assembly to rewrite the Constitution and resolve the crisis. At that time Colombia had the oldest constitution in South America. Created in 1886, it no longer met the people's needs.

César Gaviria Trujillo (right) on a visit to Japan

Elections were held, and representatives to the Assembly came from every section of society. There were former guerrillas, Native Americans, and Protestants, as well as members of the traditional Conservative and Liberal parties. The Assembly produced a Constitution that allowed members of these ethnic and minority groups to be represented in Congress for the first time.

Opposite: **The legislature in session**

The National Flag and Emblem

Colombia's flag consists of three horizontal stripes—yellow, dark blue, and red. The yellow stripe represents the gold of the New World, the red stripe stands for the blood shed for independence, and the blue stripe is for the Atlantic and Pacific Oceans.

The coat of arms, adopted in 1834, is topped by a condor. It also shows a pomegranate, horns of plenty, a liberty cap, and the Isthmus of Panama, which was once part of Colombia.

The 1991 Constitution

The Constitution is based on three branches of government: the executive, represented by the president and his cabinet; the legislative, which is made up of the Senate and the House of Representatives; and the judiciary, which is responsible for the legal administration.

The president is elected for a four-year term and cannot immediately be reelected to a second term. He has a vice president. Senators and representatives are elected in the same year as the president. The Senate has 102 directly elected members and the House of Representatives has 165 members, which include at least two representatives of each national department. There are designated seats for minority groups such as the Native Americans, who have two seats in the Senate, and blacks and guerrillas, with two seats each in the House of Representatives.

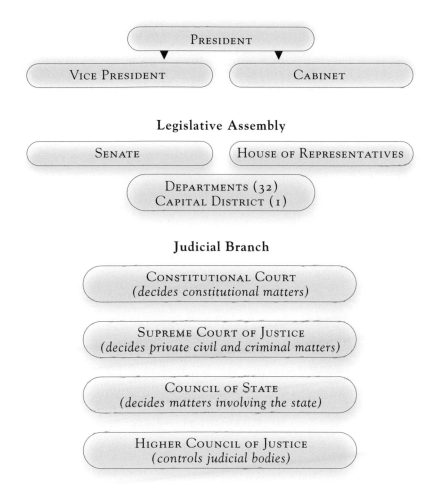

PRESIDENT

VICE PRESIDENT   CABINET

Legislative Assembly

SENATE   HOUSE OF REPRESENTATIVES

DEPARTMENTS (32)
CAPITAL DISTRICT (1)

Judicial Branch

CONSTITUTIONAL COURT
(decides constitutional matters)

SUPREME COURT OF JUSTICE
(decides private civil and criminal matters)

COUNCIL OF STATE
(decides matters involving the state)

HIGHER COUNCIL OF JUSTICE
(controls judicial bodies)

**The National Government
of Colombia**

The country is divided into thirty-two departments and one Capital District. These are subdivided into 1,011 municipalities: The governor and a legislature for each department are elected by the people. The municipalities, including the Capital District of Santafé de Bogotá, are headed by mayors.

The judiciary is headed by the Supreme Court of Justice. Judges serve one eight-year term of office. They cannot be appointed for a second term.

Internal Divisions

1 Amazonas	12 Chocó	23 Norte de Santander
2 Antioquia	13 Córdoba	24 Putumayo
3 Arauca	14 Cundinamarca	25 Quindio
4 Atlántico	15 Capital District	26 Risaralda
5 Bolívar	16 Guainia	27 San Andrés y Providencia
6 Boyacá	17 Guaviare	28 Santander
7 Caldas	18 Huila	29 Sucre
8 Caquetá	19 La Guajira	30 Tolima
9 Casanare	20 Magdalena	31 Valle del Cauca
10 Cauca	21 Meta	32 Vaupés
11 Cesar	22 Nariño	33 Vichada

The Guerrillas

For almost fifty years, guerrilla groups have played an important part in Colombian life. Some, like the *Fuerzas Armadas Revolucionarias de Colombia* (FARC; Revolutionary Armed Forces of Colombia), emerged during the years of La Violencia; others, like the *Ejército de Liberación Nacional* (ELN; Army of National Liberation), were formed after Fidel Castro's successful revolution in Cuba in 1959. *The Movimiento 19 de Abril* (M-19; April 19 Movement) came into being in the 1970s.

By the end of the 1970s, perhaps a dozen different guerrilla groups operated in rural areas where they controlled entire towns and villages. Colombia was in an almost permanent state of siege. In 1982, in the face of mounting guerrilla activity, President Belisario Betancur offered the guerrillas an amnesty.

Some guerillas did lay down their arms, and the FARC formed their own political party—the *Unión Patriótica* (UP). But the peace did not last. The UP became a target for right-wing death squads, while other guerrilla groups continued much as before, with frequent bombings and assassinations in the early 1990s.

Carlos Lleras Restrepo (1908–1994)

When he died at the age of 86, Carlos Lleras Restrepo was probably Colombia's most respected elder statesman. He had been a leading member of the Liberal Party since the 1930s and president of the country from 1966 to 1970. His presidency coincided with the National Front period, when the country was under an almost continuous state of siege. Many Colombians remember the night Lleras Restrepo announced a curfew on television. Looking at his watch, he told his audience they had twenty minutes to get home to bed!

The low point of his career was the accusation of fraudulent elections in 1970, which led to the formation of the M-19 guerrillas. They took their name, *Movimiento 19 de Abril*, from the date of the election (April 19). After he retired from politics, Lleras Restrepo worked on a history of Colombia. He had written twelve volumes when he died but the work was not finished. Today his son Carlos follows his path in national politics.

During César Gaviria Trujillo's presidency (1990–1994), there were more talks between the government and the guerrillas. As a result, two guerrilla organizations, including the M-19, agreed to stop fighting. But the others did not agree and the negotiations came to nothing. A fundamental problem was the lack of trust between the guerrillas and the military, who had fought one another for so many years. In 1992, the president called off the talks, and the bombings and assassinations began again.

In 1994 when national and local elections took place, it became apparent just how much control the guerrillas had in the countryside. Although security forces were brought in, party candidates were often unable to campaign and voters were intimidated. The result was that people with links to the guerrillas or drug dealers were voted in as mayors or councillors in many places. Councillors serve on local municipal and town councils. The government again tried to negotiate with the guerrillas after the elections, but a new wave of attacks and bombings in 1995 and 1996 put an end to those negotiations too.

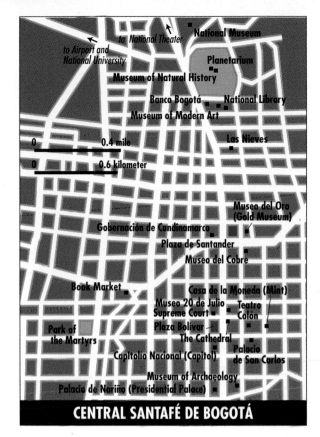

CENTRAL SANTAFÉ DE BOGOTÁ

The Drug Business

During the 1970s and 1980s, some guerrilla groups also became involved in the illegal drug trade, first with marijuana and later with cocaine. Most of the coca plants are grown in Peru and Bolivia, but Colombia has the factories that process the leaves into basic cocaine paste as well as the means to export the drugs.

Violence escalated as drug dealers became enormously wealthy and powerful, with the biggest dealers, like Pablo Escobar from Medellín, able to threaten the very existence of the national government. Although Escobar had a following among the poor, whom he helped with housing and huge charitable donations, he kept his own private army of hun-

Opposite: **M-19 guerrillas surrender their arms.**

A cocaine factory

Opposite: **The funeral procession for Luis Carlos Galán**

Drug baron Pablo Escobar

dreds of young killers to put down any opposition. This opposition included judges, politicians, and generals—and anyone else who got in his way. The harder the government tried to crush him, the more ruthlessly he fought back. The name *Escobar* became associated with almost any kind of atrocity.

Around the time of the 1990 election, three presidential candidates were assassinated, including front-runner Luis Carlos Galán. President Virgilio Barco Vargas called for an all-out war on drugs, for which he received help from the U.S. Drug Enforcement Administration (DEA) and from the British Army's Special Air Service. Hostilities reached a new level as car bombs killed hundreds. Buildings, especially security buildings, and police were targeted. In one incident, more than 100 people died when a domestic airliner was blown up. The security forces captured some leading members of the drug business.

When President César Gaviria Trujillo was elected in 1990, he took a different approach to the drug traffickers. He offered them lenient sentences in return for their surrender and cooperation. His approach appeared to be successful when Escobar and others gave themselves up. However, Escobar's time in prison was spent in considerable luxury, running his drug business from computers, faxes, and phones.

Santafé de Bogotá: Did You Know This?

Population: 6,004,782 (1996 estimate)

Year Founded: 1538, by Gonzalo Jiménez de Quesada

Altitude: 8,563 feet (2,610 m) above sea level

Average Daily Temperature: *January* 58°F (14.4°C)

                                    July 57°F (13.9°C)

Average Annual Rainfall: 32 inches (81 cm)

Then, one day in July 1992, Escobar decided to walk out. Everyone was outraged that this had been allowed to happen, and the new message from the Colombian government was that Escobar must be captured or killed at all costs. In December 1993, it finally happened. A phone call Escobar made to his son and family in Santafé de Bogotá was traced to a house in Medellín. He was killed while trying to escape after a shoot-out.

President Ernesto Samper Pizano

The major problem that President Ernesto Samper Pizano inherited when he was elected in 1994 was the drug business in Cali. Drug dealers had existed there for years, but after the death of Escobar they became the most powerful and important in Colombia. The situation was complicated by the fact that they did not use guns and violence to get what they wanted. Instead, they infiltrated the government and the security forces and hired expensive lawyers to look after their interests. The government of President Gaviria Trujillo had

The National Police on duty in Santafé de Bogotá

failed to make headway against the Cali drug traffickers, much to the frustration of the U.S. authorities. They looked to President Samper Pizano for better results.

Within months of taking office, however, Samper Pizano himself was accused of having a connection to the Cali drug runners. He furiously denied this, and a change of personnel in top security jobs eventually brought results. In 1995, some of the most important drug dealers in Cali were arrested.

Himno Nacional—"Oh Glory Unfading"

Coro	Chorus
Oh gloria inmarcesible!	Oh unfading glory!
Oh júbilo inmortal	Oh immortal joy
en surcos de dolores	In furrows of sorrow
el bien germina ya.	Good now grows.

Primera estrofa	First verse
Cesó la horrible noche	The dreadful night is over
la libertad sublime	Sublime freedom
derrama las auroras	Scatters the auroras
de su invencible luz.	Of its invincible light.
La humanidad entera,	The whole of humanity,
que entre cadenas gime	In chains wailing,
comprende las palabras	Understands the words
del que murió en la cruz.	of He who died on the cross.

Nine verses follow, with the chorus repeated after each one. Because the song is so long, only the chorus, first verse, and then a repeated chorus are usually sung. The lyrics are written by former president Rafael Núñez; the music is by Oreste Sindicí, an Italian-born Colombian.

But rumors that Samper Pizano's presidential campaign had received money from the traffickers during the 1994 elections continued until 1996, when the House of Representatives voted to absolve him of any such wrongdoing.

In 1998, the war against drugs continued as a new president was elected. However, once in office, President Andrés Pastrana's attention was turned to the guerrillas and the increasing violence within Colombia. In 2002, new President Álvaro Uribe Vélez inherited many of the same problems that his predecessor Pastrana faced.

President Álvaro Uribe Vélez

Economic Resources

Colombia is rich in mineral resources and energy sources, and has extremely fertile land. It is South America's largest producer of gold and supplies about half the world's emeralds, with stones of high quality. It has Latin America's largest deposits of coal and plentiful rivers for hydroelectricity. Its oil reserves are among the largest in the world. Most of all, Colombia is known for its coffee and is second in coffee production only to Brazil.

Coffee trees surround a coffee farm.

C OLOMBIA HAS BEEN VERGING ON CIVIL WAR SINCE THE late 1940s and has experienced horrendous problems with guerrillas and drug dealers, but it is still one of Latin America's economic success stories. It has enjoyed one of the area's highest rates of growth over the past twenty years and has significantly increased its exports.

Coffee

Coffee was introduced into Colombia as early as 1700 by Jesuit missionaries, but it did not become an important export until the 1800s. Coffee's success as an export is largely due to the energy and initiative of a group of European Jews who farmed in the Cordillera Central in what are now Antioquia and Caldas. By the end of the nineteenth century, coffee accounted for half of Colombia's exports. The industry really took off about 1910, when railroads were built to take the coffee to the ports.

At first large landowners invested in the industry, but it soon became clear that small farms were the best way to go. The finest coffee grows on

Coffee beans drying outdoors

hilly slopes at altitudes of 3,000 to 6,000 feet (914 to 1,829 m), where it is not easy to use mechanized vehicles. Small family farms took over the cultivation, and today some 350,000 families work in the coffee business.

The mountain climate is ideal for the Arabica plant, a mild variety of coffee that traditionally thrives in the shade. The coffee farmers also plant varieties that do well in open sunlight.

Their implements are traditional—the hoe and the machete—and the growers pick the coffee beans, or berries, by hand. At harvest time, the whole family pitches in. A mature tree yields about 2,000 beans a year, which, when processed, fill only a 1-pound (0.4-kg) coffee can! An experienced farmer can pick about 200 pounds (91 kg) a day.

The farmers use machines to separate the beans from the outer pulp, and the beans are then washed, graded, and dried on terraces in the sun. There are few good roads around small coffee farms, so the beans are carried by mule and donkey to the nearest mill. There they are checked and bagged for export.

Drug Money

The effects of drug money on the Colombian economy are hard to figure because the facts are not known. We can only guess. While the sums of money involved probably have been exaggerated, they very likely exceed revenue earned from coffee and other legitimate exports. The drug money is laundered mainly through certain areas of the economy, such as construction, cattle-ranching, and the import of consumer goods.

In recent years, the coffee industry has had some problems. World prices for coffee have dropped and disease has hit about half of the country's coffee bushes. Many growers are now in debt and seek government help.

Crops and Cattle

With a climate ranging from the hot, wet lowlands to the cool mountain zones, Colombia produces a wide variety of crops. Tobacco, sugar, and cacao, used for chocolate, have been grown since colonial times. Sugarcane has been concentrated in the river valleys, especially the Cauca, and on the Pacific coast. Bananas were introduced in the last century and are grown mainly on the Caribbean coast.

Heavy machinery is used to load sugarcane onto wagons for shipment.

What Colombia Grows, Makes, and Mines

Agriculture (1995)

Sugarcane	30,000,000 metric tons
Potatoes	3,200,000 metric tons
Plantains	2,890,000 metric tons

Manufacturing *(in Col$ 000,000; 1992)*

Processed food	1,160,600
Beverages	953,400
Textiles and clothing	631,700

Mining (1995)

Coal	21,713,000 metric tons
Emeralds	6,305,903 carats
Iron ore	609,615 metric tons

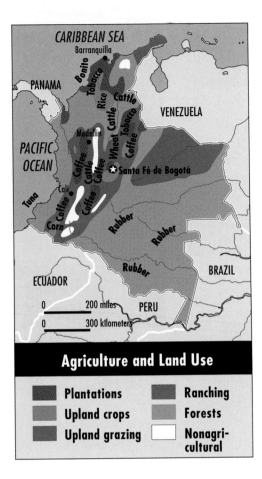

Agriculture and Land Use

- Plantations
- Upland crops
- Upland grazing
- Ranching
- Forests
- Nonagri-cultural

On the large, treeless savanna outside Santafé de Bogotá, greenhouses cover acres of land. These have been erected for the cut-flower industry, which was started in the 1970s. Today Colombia is one of the world's leading exporters of cut flowers such as roses, carnations, chrysanthemums, and orchids.

Because the best altitude for growing flowers is around 8,000 feet (2,438 m), the savanna accounts for more than 80 percent of Colombia's flower production. Medellín claims to be the world center for orchids, and its flowers are flown to the United States every day.

Flower cutters inside a greenhouse

Cattle and other livestock are also important in the agricultural economy. Most cattle are herded in the vast llanos, in the river valleys, and on the Caribbean coast. At times there have been nearly as many cattle as people in Colombia, averaging about 25 million. In the past two decades, the beef industry has

Cattle ranchers drive their herd through a river.

Money Facts

Money in Colombia is based on the *peso* (Col$). One peso is equal to 100 centavos. Pesos are issued in 100, 200, 1,000, 2,000, 5,000, 10,000, and 20,000 paper-note denominations. Coins are issued in 50 centavos and 1, 2, 5, 10, 20, and 50 pesos. In early 2003, 2,819 pesos equaled U.S.$1.

On the back of the 1,000-peso note is the *Pantano de Vargas* Monument, a huge sculpture representing that famous battle. It was the last battle before the Battle of Boyacá in 1819 led to the defeat of the Spaniards.

The battle of the *Pantano de Vargas* is famous because Bolívar's soldiers had ragged clothing, few shoes, and certainly no weapons to match the Spaniards'. Also, Bolívar's men had marched all the way from Venezuela across the llanos on foot, through freezing *páramos* and over high

mountains. Yet they still defeated the Spaniards. The marsh on which they fought is near the town of Paipa, famous for its hot springs, and the villa where Bolívar rested is now a hotel.

developed rapidly, and the leather industry is also important. The hides are used to make fashionable handbags and luggage, which are popular in Europe and North America.

Forestry and Fishing

About half of Colombia is covered by forest and woodland, much of it in inaccessible areas of the country such as the Amazon. Because of the problems of getting into such regions, the timber industry was slow to take off.

During the second half of the twentieth century, however, new roads have been built and vast tracts of forests have been cut down. Logs are floated on rivers or sent by truck to sawmills alongside the rivers. The mills produce plywood for the domestic and export markets. Large cleared areas in the forest have been converted to cattle-ranching and farming.

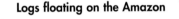

Logs floating on the Amazon

With its long coastline and many rivers, it is surprising that Colombia's fishing industry is not more developed. The most successful commercial fishing effort is shrimp farms, recently established on both the Caribbean and Pacific coasts.

Minerals

Colombia has gold, silver, platinum, copper, bauxite, iron ore, phosphates, uranium, nickel, rock salt, marble, and limestone. Colombia also has large coal deposits, the richest coalfield being the huge mining complex of El Cerrejón in the Guajira peninsula. Its high-quality hard coal is near the surface and easily mined.

A Guajiro Indian harvests a salt flat.

The most precious and valued mineral, however, is emeralds. Most come from the Muzo and Chivor mines in the department of Boyacá. Early in this century the world's largest emerald, the 632-carat Patricia, was found in Peñas Blancas in Boyacá.

In 1946 the government

nationalized the emerald mines but, despite a heavy police and army presence, they were unable to keep control. Since 1973 the emerald-mining zone has been out of the hands of the government. Much of the industry is now controlled by drug dealers and guerrilla forces, who fought violently among themselves to get it.

An emerald being cut

Panning for Gold

Much of Colombia's gold comes from the departments of Antioquia and Chocó. Many poor people are involved in panning, or searching for gold in rivers. They live and work in grim conditions in the hope that one day they will strike it rich.

Along the River Telembí in the state of Nariño, for example, the lower banks have been pretty well exhausted. People have ventured farther upriver looking for streams higher up the sides of the river valley.

The men who are panning for gold push the river banks into the water where the women have made a little dam. There they swirl the mud or sand around in shallow pans till the gold dust or nuggets, which are heavy, are left on the bottom of the pan. Many people have spent a lifetime with little success. Only a few have made a fortune.

Colombia's Systems of Weights and Measures

The metric system was introduced in 1857, but Colombians generally use Spanish weights and measures, such as the *vara* (about 28 inches, or 71 cm), the *libra* (about 1 pound, or 0.45 kg), and the *arroba* (about 25 pounds, or 11.3 kg). They measure gasoline in U.S. gallons.

The government receives money from the emerald concessions, and there have been many efforts to organize the export of gems. A gem exchange was planned for introduction in 1998. So many emeralds are removed and sent out of the country illegally, however, that no one knows for sure what the industry is worth, but at least several billion dollars are involved.

Energy

If all goes well, Colombia will become a major world oil producer early in the next millennium. The most recent discoveries have been made in the llanos, where the find at Casanare is thought to be the biggest field found in the world in the last ten years.

Oil has been exported from the nearby Arauca field since the 1980s. A 500-mile (805-km) pipeline was built over the Andes to connect the field with the coast. The pipeline has frequently been blown up by guerrillas, who are very active in the area.

Colombia also has natural gas, which is often found near oil deposits. Gas reserves have also been located in the Guajira peninsula. Hydroelectricity is another source of energy in Colombia. Experts believe that Colombia's many rivers and high rainfall have enormous potential for providing hydroelectric power.

Workers in Colombia's oil industry

Manufacturing

Manufacturing industries are a major source of work in many towns. Factories manufacture tires, processed food and drinks, transport equipment, and pharmaceutical and chemical products. Medellín is the heart of the textile industry. It also has brickworks and makes leather goods and plastics. Publishing is one of Colombia's newest industries, with many companies based in Cali. They have been very successful with "pop-up" and illustrated books.

Cost of Living

	Col$	U.S.$
2.2 pounds (1 kg) sugar	820	.57
2.2 pounds (1 kg) coffee	2,700	1.87
2.2 pounds (1 kg) flour	620	.43
2.2 pounds (1 kg) rice	1,100	.76
2.2 pounds (1 kg) beans	3,400	2.36
2.2 pounds (1 kg) fish	4,300	2.98
2.2 pounds (1 kg) meat	5,600	3.88
2 quarts (1l) milk	980	.68
one egg	140	.10

U.S.$1 = 1,443 pesos (1998)

People of Colombia

Nearly 37 million people live in Colombia, giving it the second-largest population in South America, after Brazil. Most of the Native Americans who lived there when the Spaniards arrived died or disappeared within a few decades of the conquest. Today, Native Americans represent no more than 1 percent of the population.

Mestizo and mulato youths in Cartagena

M ORE THAN HALF OF COLOMBIANS are *mestizos*, the mixed-race descendants of Native Americans and Europeans. They form the largest group and the bulk of the middle class and the working class. The next-largest group are whites, mainly descendants of the Spanish settlers or other Europeans who arrived as immigrants in the nineteenth and twentieth centuries.

Less than 20 percent of Colombia's population are blacks or *mulatos*—people of mixed black and European parentage. The other tiny group that makes up the population are *zambos*—people born into mixed black and Native American families.

Unlike most countries in South America, Colombia does not have a huge capital city that dominates the country. In addition to Santafé de Bogotá, with a population of about 6 million, Colombia has two cities in the highlands with populations of about 2 million each—Cali and Medellín. Barranquilla, on the Caribbean coast, has about 1 million people. Another 37 cities have over 100,000 people each.

In recent years, many people have moved from rural areas into towns, partly through fear of the guerrillas and partly in

Who Lives in Colombia?	
Mestizos	58%
Whites	20%
Mulatos	14%
Blacks	4%
Zambos	3%
Native Americans	1%

Opposite: **A mulato boy carrying fried papaya**

People of Colombia **85**

Population of Major Cities (1997 est.)	
Bogotá	6,004,782
Cali	1,985,906
Medellín	1,970,691
Barranquilla	1,157,826
Cartagena	812,595

People move to the cities in search of a better way of life.

search of a better way of life. The number of people living in towns rose from 65 percent in 1985 to 73 percent in 1993.

Today, more than 80 percent of the population live in the highlands. The llanos and the Amazon, which together cover two-thirds of the country, have less than 2 percent of the people.

Mestizos and Whites

Most of the people in the highlands are mestizos and whites. Whites can be distinguished by their lighter skin or by their names because a few are directly related to the first Spanish settlers. As a group, they have retained their higher social position, working primarily in government or holding important business positions.

The largely middle- and working-class mestizos live and work like people in any Western city. Their employment ranges from the professions, including lawyers, teachers, and doctors, to work in banks and offices, to trading in import and export businesses and stores. Some work as taxi drivers or domestic servants or by trading trinkets, cigarettes, sweets, and other items from street stalls.

Mestizos dress like other city workers, in business suits or jeans and shirts, depending on their job. The kind of house they live in depends on their income. While the working and middle classes generally live in modern apartment buildings or in subsidized housing, poor people live in shanty towns on the outskirts of the cities, often without electricity or running water.

The contrast between their run-down shacks and the affluent suburbs of the rich demonstrates the huge gap between rich and poor. Wealthy people live in luxurious, detached houses protected by guards, dogs, and wire fences. They have many servants and large grounds.

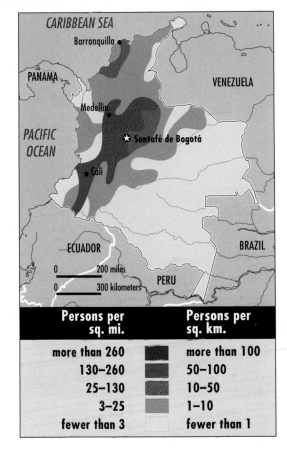

Persons per sq. mi.		Persons per sq. km.
more than 260		more than 100
130–260		50–100
25–130		10–50
3–25		1–10
fewer than 3		fewer than 1

A textile plant manager of Spanish descent in Medellín

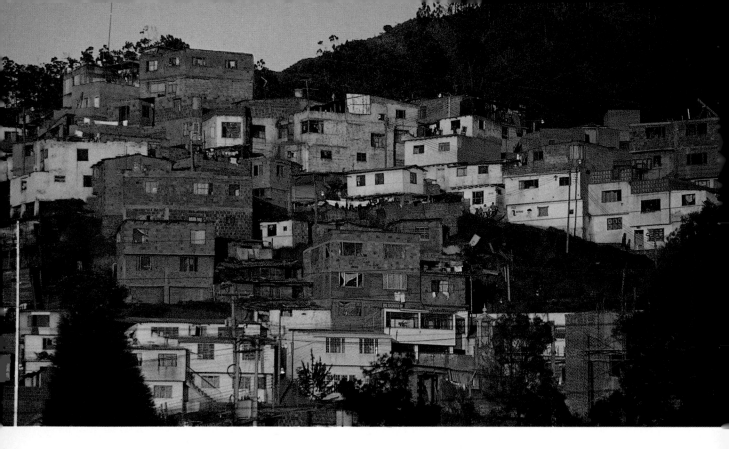

Some shanty towns have no electricity or running water.

Colombian society is quite rigid, and traditionally it has been difficult to move from one social level to another. Even though the drug dealers have incredible amounts of money, they have not been able to cross social barriers. Although money and influence play a greater part today in dictating social positions, the drug traffickers will never be fully accepted.

Antioqueños

Relatively few immigrants have come to Colombia compared with other South American countries. The most important group were the Jewish refugees from Spain who settled in the little valley of the Rió Aburra in the Cordillera Central in the early seventeenth century.

At first they farmed the hillsides with maize, beans, sugarcane, and fruit. They did the work themselves, largely without help from mestizos, blacks, or mulatos, and they married within their own community. They founded Medellín in 1616. Needing more land, in the early nineteenth century they cleared trees from the western slopes of the Cordillera Central, cultivated coffee, and became very successful.

The energy and drive of these pioneers turned the region into the economic and industrial heartland of Colombia. Today, the departments of Antioquia and Caldas produce half of Colombia's coffee crop. The industrialization of Medellín followed the coffee boom, and today that city produces 80 percent of the country's textiles. Its industrial activity also includes brick-making, leather goods, and plastics. The *paisas*, as Antioqueños are known locally, continue to be the driving force behind the commercial success of the region.

Enjoying a cup of coffee in Antioquia

Blacks and Mulatos

It has been estimated that about 1 million black slaves passed through Cartagena. From there they went to work on sugarcane plantations along the Caribbean coast and in the Magdalena and Cauca river valleys. Some were sent to the Chocó gold mines, and others to different parts of South America. Their

Spanish Pronunciation

Spanish is Colombia's official language and is spoken by everyone except a few tribes in remote areas. Colombians claim to speak the purest form of Spanish. The main variation is on the Caribbean coast, where people speak more quickly and with a regional accent.

The Spanish alphabet has 28 letters. It does not use k or w, but does include ch, ll, ñ, and rr.

Spanish vowels are always pronounced the same way:

a as in car	i as in ice	u as in rude
e as in pet	o as in sow	

Consonants are similar to those in English but with some exceptions:

- b and v sound the same
- c is like "s" before "e" and "i"
- ch as in "charm"
- d within a word is pronounced "th," except after "l" and "n," when it is like the "d" in "desk"
- h is not pronounced in Spanish words
- j has no exact equivalent in English but is like an "h" spoken from the throat
- ll is similar to "y" in yawn
- ñ sounds like "ny" with "y" pronounced as a consonant, as in "canyon"
- qu replaces the "k" sound
- rr is strongly rolled

Odd Expressions

A *lagarto* (lizard) is a person who wants to become high class by meeting important people but who makes those people uncomfortable.

A *sardina* or a *sardino* (a sardine—a fish) is a very young girl or boy.

A *voltiarepas* is a person who is always changing sides. It comes from two words. *Voltear* means "to turn over," and *arepas* is a corn griddle pancake popular in Colombia.

Vale huevo means, literally, "It is worth an egg," or, figuratively, "It doesn't matter."

¡Es un verraco! means "He's great!" or "He's very courageous!" *Verraco* means "pig" or "boar." The expression used to be an insult.

descendants still live in these regions, with the greatest number of blacks in the Chocó.

In the Magdalena and Cauca river valleys, many blacks and mulatos still work on sugarcane plantations or in sugarcane-processing plants. Some have small farms where they grow rice, tobacco, coffee, and cotton, while others work on cattle ranches. On the Caribbean coast, most of the workers on the banana plantations are blacks or mulatos. The port of Buenaventura is the main source of employment in the Chocó, though people outside town earn a living fishing or by growing basic crops such as *yuca*, bananas, or beans.

Blacks and mulatos, like other people from rural areas, have a tough time when they move into the towns. They find it difficult to get work or a decent home and tend to remain at the lowest level of society. There is more opportunity for educated blacks or mulatos, but few have made it to the top political or commercial jobs.

Native Americans

Some 50 different groups of Native Americans live in Colombia. They belong to several linguistic families of which the most common are Arawak, Chibchan, Carib, and Tupi-Guaraní. About 200 native dialects are still used.

Many blacks and mulatos work in the sugarcane industry.

The Guajiro

The Guajiro (also known as Wayu or Wayuu) number between 60,000 and 80,000. They are the largest Native American group in the lowlands of South America.

The Guajiro live in the Guajira peninsula, a harsh place with a hot, dry, barren landscape. It is the location of Colombia's largest coal mine, and salt is also mined there. There are few roads on the peninsula and virtually no transport.

Nevertheless, for decades this area has been the center of illegal trade, most recently drugs. Some Guajiro have benefited from this illegal activity, earning cash as truck drivers or

Names

Last names are very important in Colombia. Everybody has two last names. Usually, the first last name is the father's last name, and the second last name is the mother's. People generally usually use both of their last names.

Children are often given two or three names, mainly to keep the names of loved ones in the family. An English name is considered to be "posh" and is also used because of the popularity of "American" style. Antioqueños like to call children by the English version of a name. John, for example, is popular, but used with another name like Jairo. John-Jairo is typical. Even before Princess Diana's death, a popular name was Lady-Diana López, for example, but spelled Lady-dayana.

Names that include María are widely used, like Ana-María, María de la Paz, María del Carmen, María Luisa, and María José. For boys, many "double" names include Juan or José; for example, Juan Pablo, Juan Carlos, and José María. Many names honor saints, like José (Saint Joseph), María (the Virgin Mary), Juan (Saint John), and even Jesús. The combination of Jesús-María is used for boys.

Nicknames are popular too. Some names have their corresponding nickname: José is Pepe; Francisco is Pacho; Jesús is Chucho; Luis is Lucho.

handling cargo. Unfortunately, they have also been introduced to guns and alcohol.

But most Guajiro have kept to their traditional life of herding and farming. Their cattle are their most prized possessions, and their seminomadic lifestyle is dictated by the animals' needs. A family group is known as a *casta*, and it is important for a casta to own as many animals as possible. Animals are so well treated that a shaman is called in when an animal is ill.

The peninsula is desperately short of water despite efforts by the government to install reservoirs. Rain falls only between September and December, and then very lightly, so the Guajiro keep on the move to find water and grazing land. As they move across the desert they erect temporary shelters of cactus branches. Their permanent homes are made of woven twigs plastered with clay and roofed with cactus. Some homes are brick with corrugated iron roofs.

Guajiro men wear shirts and trousers, but women's clothing is designed to protect them from the fierce sun. They wear long, flowing, brightly colored robes called *mantas*, cover their heads with a cloth, and paint their faces with a mixture of goat fat and charcoal. They wear sandals with a large pom-pom. Their main decoration is a necklace called a *tuma*, made of semi-precious stones and passed from mother to daughter.

A Guajiro nomad weaving a hammock

The Arhuaco and the Kogi

The Arhuaco and the Kogi live in the Sierra Nevada de Santa Marta and are thought to be descendants of the Tayrona. The Arhuaco are a much larger group, numbering perhaps 5,000. They have had more contact with outsiders, including missionaries. Some have adopted Western ways and moved to the lowlands, where they live by trading.

The Kogi reject outsiders and if necessary move away, deeper into the mountains. Because of their isolation, the Kogi have kept many of their age-old traditions. A typical Kogi village has a hut for men in the center, with smaller huts surrounding it for women and children. Most huts are round with thatched, cone-shaped roofs that resemble the nearby mountains. The snow-covered peaks that surround their villages are sacred to the Kogi, who believe that the Sierra Nevada is the center of the universe.

The people do not live in these settlements. They use them only for communal meetings or celebrations. The Kogi are deeply spiritual, and the most important people are the priests, or *mamas*. Mamas decide all family and community matters and call all the people to the village when there are problems to be resolved.

Most of the time the Kogi farm the mountain slopes, where each family owns land at different levels. They grow potatoes, manioc, corn, and fruit. They also cultivate sugar, which they sell or exchange for utensils such as knives or metal pots. They use the tough fiber of the agave plant to make hammocks, nets, bags, and ropes. Kogi dress is a simple cotton tunic, usu-

ally knee-length, and worn by the men over loosely woven pants. They also have sombrero-style hats. Pointed hats may only be worn by the mamas.

A typical Kogi village

Threatened Tribes

The last few members of the Barí tribe, or Motilones, live in the Sierra de Perijá in the northernmost part of the Cordillera Oriental. Once this tribe was widespread, but they suffered like other Indians from the Spanish conquest.

The almost final blow, however, was the discovery of oil on their land in the 1920s. Settlers and speculators crowded into the area, driving the Indians from their homes. The Barí fought back and many died. The survivors moved higher into the mountains. But even the few hundred Barí who survived are not safe, as outsiders want their land and continue to invade their territory.

The discovery of oil also caused the near-demise of the Guahibo tribe, whose home is the llanos. For centuries they were a seminomadic people living peacefully alongside the horsemen herding cattle across the great plains. But when rumors of oil began, large land investors moved in and tried to eject the Guahibo. The Indians retaliated, eventually forming their own movement for self-defense, which at times became militant. In response, the landowners called in the government and the army, and the Guahibo were overwhelmed. Many people protested the government's actions, but nothing was changed.

The Paéz and the Guambiano

Mestizos are not the only people who live in the southern highlands. Native Americans include the Paéz and the Guambiano. They are both Chibcha-speaking people and probably number about 50,000.

They live by farming. With simple wooden implements and ox-drawn plows, they cultivate crops on the hilly slopes. They grow enough for their family and a small surplus to sell in local markets. They keep some animals, including turkeys and sheep. The women also weave, using cotton and wool to make garments and handicrafts that they sell locally.

It is a hard life in the high cold regions of the mountains, and the traditional chewing of coca leaves helps to dull the effects of cold and hunger. Warm clothes are essential too. People wrap themselves in large woolen *ruanas*—like ponchos but open down the front—to keep warm. The traditional dress of the Guambiano women is strikingly colorful, with deep-blue long skirts and ruanas. They wear many strings of white beads around the neck. Men wear a kind of long skirt with a small rectangular poncho and a hat that may be round like a derby or flat like a mortarboard.

Although these groups are still independent, their way of life is changing as they have more contact with mestizos. Some now prefer Western clothing and buy consumer goods such as bicycles, transistor radios, and metal pots and pans. And many people now send their children to the local schools to learn Spanish.

Chocó and Amazon Forest Peoples

Though their homelands are far apart, the Chocó and the Amazon forest people have similar lifestyles. Both regions have dense rain forests and numerous rivers. In the forests, people cut down and burn trees to clear patches for basic crops like manioc, plantains, and peanuts.

Guambiano schoolchildren

The Caribbean Islands

The first inhabitants of San Andrés and Providencia *(right)* were Dutch. In 1631 they were moved away by the English, who introduced black slaves from Jamaica. The islands were then used as a base by pirates who attacked the Spanish galleons. The infamous pirate Henry Morgan is said to have hidden treasure on San Andrés. After the pirates left, the islands were inhabited by a few English settlers and some blacks from Caribbean islands.

Colombia claimed the islands after it became independent but Nicaragua, which is much closer to them, objected. The dispute was settled in a 1928 treaty, and until the 1950s the islands were basically English in language, culture, and traditions.

Change came with regular air flights and shipping to and from the Colombian mainland. In recent years, thousands of Colombians from the mainland have settled in the islands. Spanish is now as common as English, and where the population once was mainly Protestant, today many are Roman Catholic.

The forest provides all the wood and thatch the Indians need for building their homes, as well as the animals they need for meat. Sometimes they weave wild cotton to make simple clothing. They also use many forest plants to treat the sick. Rivers teem with a wide variety of fish, which men traditionally catch with nets, basket traps, spears, and lines. Dugout canoes, their main form of transport, are made of hollowed-out tree trunks.

Fiestas, when the people celebrate their spiritual beliefs, are an important part of tribal life. The forest people believe in contact with the supernatural through their shamans, and their gods are related to the natural world around them. At fiesta time, they paint their bodies, dance, and play music on drums and reed or bamboo flutes.

The main tribes of the Chocó are the Noanama, Cuna, Embera, and Catio. Amazon tribes include the Tukano, Huitoto, Barasana, and Cofan. Many of these people, particularly in the Chocó, share similar problems. Their lands and way of life are threatened by people who are destroying the forest to clear land for farming and ranching, or for the timber trade.

Noanama travel
the waters of the Chocó by
dugout canoe.

Opposite: A Cofan woman weaving a bag

Spiritual Life

Roman Catholicism was brought to Colombia by Spanish missionaries at the time of the conquest. After independence, the Catholic Church became a powerful organization. It was associated with the Conservatives, the party that represented wealth and large landowners. At that time the church opposed other religions, which were seen as a threat to its status and power.

THE LIBERALS OPPOSED THESE views. When they came into power in the 1860s and 1870s, they reduced the power of the church by taking away its lands and allowing people to choose their own religion. When the Conservatives returned to power, they introduced the 1886 Constitution in which the status of the church and its authority over education were restored.

The interior of a Catholic church in Pasto

In 1973, the church relinquished some of its control over education. In 1976, it agreed to legal divorce for certain cases. It was not until the 1991 Constitution that divorce became possible for all marriages, whether civil or religious.

For many years Colombia has been, and perhaps still is, the most devoutly Catholic country in South America. It is perhaps significant that the first-ever papal visit to Latin America was Pope Paul VI's visit to Colombia in 1968. In the mid-1980s, some 97.5 percent of the population counted themselves as Catholic. This included the black and mulato population, as well as Native Americans. Many of these small

Religions of Colombia	
Roman Catholics	90%
Protestants, Jews, and followers of traditional native religions	10%

Opposite: **Easter celebrations in Popayán attract visitors from all over Colombia.**

Huge crowds greeted Pope
Paul VI on his 1968 visit to
Colombia.

groups, however, while considering themselves Catholic, kept
their native spiritual beliefs too. A large percentage of non-
Catholics were the Protestant population of the Caribbean
islands. There were also small numbers of Muslims, Buddhists,
Hindus, Baha'is, and Jews.

Recently there have been changes. A number of evan-
gelical groups and missionaries have been working in many
South American countries, including Colombia. The evan-
gelicals have been particularly successful among the poor in
Colombia, and it is estimated that over the past five years
the Catholic Church there has lost some 3 million followers,
or roughly 10 percent of the population. Jehovah's
Witnesses, Mormons, Calvinists, and Lutherans are among
the new religious groups in Colombia.

Celebrations and Churches

Most of Colombia's national holidays are religious, including Christmas, Easter, and Corpus Christi. The Easter celebrations in the beautiful colonial city of Popayán attract visitors from all over Colombia and neighboring countries. In elaborate processions, statues of all the city's saints are paraded through the streets. Many villages and towns throughout Colombia also celebrate their special saint's day, with parades, processions, bell-ringing, music, and dancing.

Colombia has some fine churches, convents, and monasteries. Two of the most extraordinary are the Salt Cathedral at Zipaquirá and the spectacular shrine of Las Lajas.

A huge mountain of salt stands next to the town of Zipaquirá, just over 30 miles (50 km) north of Santafé de

National Religious Holidays

Epiphany	January 6
St. Joseph's Day	March 19
Holy Thursday	March or April
Good Friday	March or April
Easter	March or April
Corpus Christi	June
Saints Peter and Paul Day	June 29
Assumption Day	August 15
All Saints Day	November 1
Immaculate Conception Day	December 8
Christmas	December 25

A corridor in the underground salt cathedral near Zipaquirá

Bogotá. This area has Colombia's richest salt mines, which have been worked since Muisca times. Inside the mountain of salt is an amazing underground cathedral hewn out of salt. It was built by miners in honor of their patron saint, *Nuestra Señora del Rosario* (Our Lady of the Rosary). The vaulted interior of the cathedral can hold at least 10,000 people and rises to about 80 feet (24 m). The altar is a solid block of salt, said to weigh 18 tons. A few years ago the walls began to crack and the cathedral was closed down while another one, even deeper in the ground, is being completed.

The Sanctuary of Our Lady of Las Lajas is a Gothic-style church built on a bridge over a very deep river gorge near the Ecuadorean border. According to legend, an image of the Virgin Mary appeared high on the steep rocks above the bridge in the eighteenth century. The church was built in 1803 to commemorate the event. It was rebuilt early this century with a spectacular design that incorporates the rock with the image as part of the high altar. Many pilgrims visit Las Lajas, leaving plaques that describe miracles that have occurred and giving thanks to the Virgin.

Kogi Beliefs

Kogi religious beliefs relate to their idea of the universe. They see the cosmos as an egg-shaped space with seven points, which include north, south, east, and west. The four cardinal points are occupied by the mythical ancestors of the Kogi. In the north are the opossum and the armadillo; in the south, the puma and the deer; in the east, the jaguar and the peccary; and in the west, the eagle and the snake.

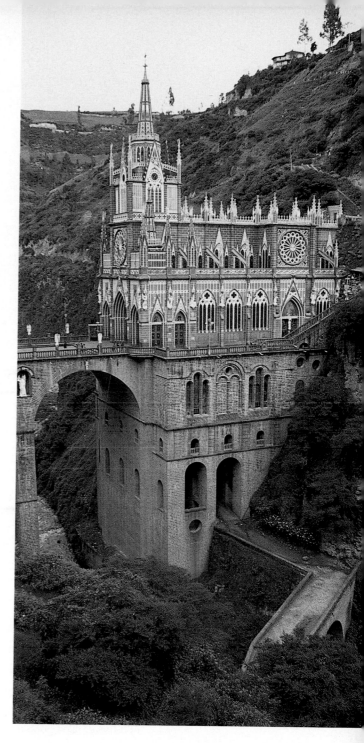

The Sanctuary of Our Lady of Las Lajas

San Pedro Claver

In Cartagena, the Cathedral and Convent of San Pedro Claver honors the priest known as the "Apostle of the Blacks" or the "Slave of the Slaves," who devoted his life to the slaves brought from Africa. He was the first person to be canonized in the New World, and his body now lies in a glass coffin beneath the high altar in the church.

The convent is a huge three-story building with arched cloisters surrounding a palm- and flower-filled patio *(above)*. It is said that the priest used to sit in a room where he could see the ships from Africa come into the harbor. Almost before the ships could be tied up, he was on the dock to comfort the slaves.

The cosmic space is divided into nine layers. The nine layers are the nine daughters of the mother goddess who created the universe, and each represents a certain kind of earth, from barren sand to rich soil. The world we live in is represented by the fifth daughter—the fertile black soil in which we cultivate our crops.

The main task of the *mamas*, or priests, is to carry out rituals to keep order in the universe. The mamas are not just shamans or witch doctors. They spend years learning tribal customs and priestly functions. The Kogi believe that mamas are responsible for the rising and setting of the sun, for the seasons, and for ensuring that the world and its people are fertile.

When the men get together in their village hut, mamas take charge of the meetings, which can last for two or three days. Meetings are also held in remote, high places in the mountains. Offerings of stones, seeds, shells, or pieces of thread, cotton, or hair are made. Sometimes there are masked dancers and the music of flutes, seed-rattles, and small drums.

The Noanama *Hai*

When they are very young, Noanama children from the Chocó are given a small wooden figure as a toy. Later their parents tell them the significance of the sacred figure, which represents their spiritual guide, or *haí*. Parents make sure the children take care of the haí, for it must never be lost. The Noanama always carry their haí with them, believing it will protect them from evil and from the vengeful spirits of wild animals.

Creativity and Sports

The early civilizations in Colombia left a rich cultural heritage. Skilled potters made hundreds of pots and clay figures. They decorated the pots with drawings of animals and birds painted in reds and black from natural earth colors. Zigzag designs with a variety of dots and whorls were favorites. Music was made on panpipes, some made of reeds and others of gold.

T HE ANCIENT GOLDSMITHS CREATED EXQUISITE OBJECTS OF thinly beaten gold. They used sophisticated techniques for shaping the molten metal. The craftspeople portrayed the ideas of their time and left no doubt that the spirits and the local rulers were all-powerful. Ceremonies such as that of

Opposite: **A cumbia dance band practices in Cartagena.**

The Gold Museum

Colombia's ancient artistic heritage is held safely in the Gold Museum in Santafé de Bogotá. The museum is arranged in three levels. The first tells the story of the early peoples who inhabited the land. Next comes the crafts and way of life of the tribes. And, finally, we see their goldwork.

Case after case of gold objects, such as masks, breast-plates, animal figures, ornaments, and drinking vessels, fill the rooms. One case contains a tiny golden raft complete with the chieftain surrounded by nobles. The collection is price-less. In the grand finale, the lights dim, you enter a darkened strong room, and the heavy door closes behind you. As the lights are turned up, thousands of golden objects glitter from every side—the fabu-lous Gold of El Dorado.

El Dorado involved hundreds of golden objects, and many of the rulers were buried with their gold masks and other finery.

Modern Colombian artists are just as creative as those of the past, and some still work with the old materials. In Santafé de Bogotá, the leading artistic jewelers make gold objects using

Los Musicos, by Fernando Botero

ancient methods. Fine necklaces, bracelets, clasps, and pins are often studded with glistening emeralds. At a simpler level, the folk artists of Pasto in the south use a traditional, natural varnish to create patterns on wooden vases, plates, stools, and tabletops.

The most famous contemporary artist is Fernando Botero. Born in 1932 to a humble family in Medellín, he was writing about art by the time he was seventeen. In 1951, he moved to Santafé de Bogotá, where he won prizes and held exhibitions. He traveled to Europe to study and then moved to New York. In 1973, he moved to Paris, where

he produced bronze sculpture. His paintings, many with bulbous inflated figures from all walks of life, command high prices everywhere. His huge sculptures, also of people and animals with bulbous shapes, are found in many of the world's major cities.

Colombia has many art galleries, including more than 100 in Santafé de Bogotá alone. Young artists are encouraged and

Gabriel García Márquez

One of the great figures of modern literature, 1982 Nobel Prize–winner Gabriel García Márquez was born in Aracataca on March 6, 1928. Aracataca is a small town in the "banana belt," the great plantations west of the Sierra Nevada de Santa Marta. The banana industry was run by an American company, so politics and economics were part of young Gabriel's daily life.

Stories of the great massacre of banana workers in March 1928 in Ciénaga were still around as he grew up. Some of the background of his life and an account of the massacre are threaded into his classic work *One Hundred Years of Solitude*.

Another well-known novel, *Love in the Time of Cholera*, is based on a family courtship. His recent works include *The General in His Labyrinth*, based on the liberator Simón Bolívar; *Love and Other Demons*, set in eighteenth-century Cartagena; and *News of a Kidnapping*, about drugs and kidnapping.

promoted at home and abroad by businesses and by the government. They work in many forms, from painting to music, writing, and poetry.

Carnivals

Barranquilla is where the young writer "Gabo" García Márquez attended school and later married his wife, Mercedes. It is a lively Caribbean city and port that once a year leaves

Carnival in Barranquilla

every care behind with its Carnival—the Mardi Gras of South America. The Carnival is a time for fun and eating before the deprivations of Lent.

In Barranquilla, the Carnival has become an exuberant ethnic mix of rhythm and color that fills the streets with processions, tableaus, and beauty queens. Parties last for days with nonstop music, masked dancers, and endless rum or *aguardiente*, a strong spirit made from sugar cane. A *parranda* or "night out" with a group of friends is an event never to be missed.

Another well-known festival, *Fiesta de Negros y Blancos* (Festival of Blacks and Whites), takes place in Pasto on January 5 and 6. January 5 is the *Día de los Negros* (Day of the Black Ones), and January 6 is the *Día de los Blancos* (Day of the White Ones). This festival probably has its roots in the celebration of the day when Christ revealed himself to the

People of all ages enjoy the Festival of Blacks and Whites in Pasto.

Three Wise Men. The origins of Pasto's festival go back to the time of Spanish rule, when slaves were allowed to celebrate on January 5. Their masters showed approval by painting their faces black. The next day, the slaves painted their faces white. Today, the boys of the town chase the girls, dabbing their faces with black shoe polish.

A Religious Wedding

When the bride arrives at the church, the bridegroom and his mother are waiting near the altar. The traditional wedding march announces the bride's arrival as she walks in by her father's side. The groom's father, the bride's mother, and the best man then enter the church. All the women stand to the left of the bride while the men stand to the right of the groom. The priest conducts the Mass, and after the Epistle is read the couple are married. Everyone then leaves the church and heads for the reception.

Music

Colombian music varies from region to region and combines many elements. The best known are the Afro-Colombian *cumbias* from the coastal regions. They are popular throughout Latin America.

The traditional cumbia groups are the *conjunto de cumbia*, whose instruments are mainly percussion, and the *conjunto de gaitas*, which uses two flutes, percussion, and maracas. Maracas are gourds containing a handful of small pebbles that give a sharp, rattling sound when shaken. The gaitas have origins in the music of Native Americans in the Sierra Nevada de Santa Marta. Cumbias have also been commercialized, with the "big band" sound accompanying major singers.

The purest form of black music in South America comes from Colombia's Pacific coast. Typical instruments are the marimba, which is similar to a xylophone with keys made of hard palm wood, and the *guasá*, a rattle containing seeds. The musicians also play many different types of drums.

Vallenatos are like folk stories set to music. The traditional vallenato has lyrics that tell love stories and dramatic tales. It is accompanied by bongo drums and a *guacharaca*, a tubular piece of wood with an irregular surface that is scratched with a small metallic fork, or a *totuma*—a hollow dried pumpkin scratched with a similar instrument. Nowadays the lyrics and music of the vallenato have changed, but some young pop-music artists like Carlos Vives are trying to revive the traditional vallenato.

The *bambuco*, the national dance, is usually accompanied by a variety of stringed instruments including the *tiple*, a small twelve-stringed guitar. The music from the open plains of the llanos is played on harps and on the *cuatro*, a four-stringed guitar.

Cycling Heroes

Cochise Rodriquez was a world champion cyclist and a national hero. He came from a poor family and made it to the top by sheer individual effort and courage. Another such cyclist was "Lucho" Herrera (right), champion of the Tour of Spain and the Tour of Italy, and winner in mountain-cycling in the Tour de France. He was nicknamed *El jardinerito* (The little gardener) because he was a gardener in Fusagasugá. Traveling up and down the steep mountain roads with his heavy gardener's bicycle gave him strength and endurance.

Sports

Soccer has become Colombia's international sporting strength since its team qualified for the finals of the last two World Cup competitions. That team was coached by Francisco Maturana, an Afro-Colombian dentist from the

Members of a boys' baseball team in training

Chocó. The sport is followed with wild enthusiasm by thousands of supporters who watch with groups of friends, often crowded around the family television set. Bars and restaurants are packed with cheering fans of both sides. When a local or national team has scored a victory, the streets are filled with a procession of cars and a constant hooting of horns.

In Colombia you can take part in almost every kind of outdoor sport. Facilities for most indoor sports are there for people who can afford them. Bullfighting, introduced by the Spanish, is very popular. The bullrings in most cities have room for thousands of spectators.

Famous Soccer Moments

Colombia beat Argentina in Buenos Aires in 1993 by 5 goals to 0. Before the game, the famous Argentinian player Maradona boasted that he was absolutely certain Argentina would beat Colombia very easily. This made Argentina's defeat even more embarrassing. Colombia's victory was celebrated like a national holiday, with parties in every house all over Colombia.

A much less happy occasion was Colombia's 2–1 defeat by the United States in the first round of the 1994 World Cup. Following successes like their defeat of Argentina, Colombia had become one of the favorites for the cup. The defeat was even more humiliating because the deciding goal was scored for the United States by Colombia's Andrés Escobar (at left in photo). It almost certainly cost him his life. He was gunned down on his return to Colombia.

Day In, Day Out

Daily life in Colombia varies from region to region. In the tropical lowlands of the Amazon and the Caribbean and Pacific coasts, most people work as fishers, small farmers, dockers, or lumbermen. A few may be gold panners or miners. Life is casual and laid back in the hot, wet climate. People wear T-shirts and shorts or jeans.

THINGS ARE NOT SO DIFFERENT ON the sugarcane plantations in the river valleys, where the climate is similar. The horsemen, or *vaqueros*, of the llanos have a tougher time, however. They spend long, hard days out on the grasslands herding cattle. The sun beats down and there is little to relieve the monotony.

The Andes are a different world. High in the cordilleras, life is equally difficult. A family with a small plot of land toils from dawn to dusk using only an ox-drawn plow and wooden tools. They have few luxuries and local fiestas are their main relaxation.

Fishers on the Guajira peninsula haul in their nets.

Opposite: **Passengers ride atop a packed *chiva* bus.**

Horsemen of the llanos spend long days in the saddle.

This hair stylist in Santafé de Bogotá received a loan to start her business.

Elsewhere on the slopes, coffee workers have a more comfortable lifestyle. The National Federation of Coffee Growers has helped them to get electricity, running water, hospitals, schools, and some good roads.

Colombia's cities are much like cities in other lands. The streets are bustling with businesspeople and fashionable shops. Long lines of traffic create ever more pollution. Vendors who cannot afford to rent shops set up stalls in the markets and along the sidewalks to sell their wares—everything from cigarettes to confetti.

City streets are also home to countless children who have left home because their families cannot afford to keep them. Street children called *gamines* live by begging or by running errands, washing cars, cleaning shoes, or anything else they

Homeless children sleep in the open.

can turn their hand to. Many become involved in drugs and crime. They sleep on the streets. Occasionally, the authorities decide to have a "clean-up" and use violent means to get rid of them. The *Niños de los Andes* (Children of the Andes) organization, set up by engineer Jaime Jaramillo to help these children, estimates that there are about 5,000 homeless children sleeping on the streets of Santafé de Bogotá.

Family Life

Letting a child live on the streets is a tragedy for a Colombian family. Families in Colombia are very close and loyal. Several generations often live in one house, and young married couples often live with their parents for a time.

Families are still quite large, although birth control is now more widely accepted. Almost everyone has an extended family that includes many relatives as well as many friends who

Tejo, or *turmequé*, is a game played by older children and adults. A heavy round metal piece is thrown about 25 feet (8 m) at a target. The target consists of several red triangles filled with gunpowder on a round metal surface covered with clay. When the target is hit, it explodes.

Another game is played with a *rana*, a wooden box. The box has a number of slots in the top, marked by numbers of 100 to 500, and a brass frog at the back with the highest number—1,000. Each player gets five brass rings to throw and tries to score the highest number.

act like godparents. Relatives stay in close touch, often visiting one another's houses.

Education

All Colombian children from 6 to 12 years old are expected to attend school. Primary school lasts for six or seven years. No one can go to secondary school without completing primary school. After secondary school, students can move on to higher education. Schooling is free, but there are also private and church-run schools. Colombia also has many universities, technical colleges, and other institutions of higher education.

Most children in Colombia today have access to a school, but the level of education they receive depends largely on where they live. The best schools are in cities and towns,

Schoolgirls visit an archaeological museum.

where there are enough teachers, classrooms, books, and equipment. Some schools have to run in shifts, with the younger children attending in the mornings and the older students in the afternoons or evenings.

In rural areas, schools may be several miles away. Children then have to walk long distances to school as there is not much public transport. Sometimes children do not go to school because their parents need them to help work on the land. Worst off are the children in remote areas like the Amazon, the Chocó, and the llanos. Some missionary schools help in these areas too, but there is the added problem that Spanish is not the first language in some communities.

One way of reaching children in remote areas has been through radio, and occasionally television. Regular educational broadcasts are now aimed at adults who have received no schooling. These broadcasts have helped to reduce illiteracy. Fifty years ago, almost 50 percent of people over ten years of age could not read or write. Today, the number has dropped to about 9 percent.

News and Communications

The Andean cordilleras have always been a huge barrier to traveling from one side of Colombia to another. Until this century, with the coming of the telephone and the airplane, frequent contact was impossible. Today, almost everyone in

Driving in Colombia

A Colombian will tell you that driving in Colombia is almost a sport, like a rally. Even basic traffic rules are not respected. There are no particular driving customs, and not much courtesy, logic, or common sense either. Strangely enough, the traffic seems to get better when the traffic lights are not working! Speed limits are exceptionally low: 37 miles (60 km) per hour on the highway, 19 miles (30 km) per hour in the city, and 25 miles (40 km) per hour on roads outside the cities. No one pays attention to speed limits, and the police do not fine people for speeding.

Colombia has access to radio, and television reaches about 90 percent of the population.

Colombia has always recognized freedom of the press officially, but several leading national papers are associated with political parties. *El Espectador*, founded in the 1880s, and *El Tiempo*, founded in 1911, are Liberal, while *La República* and *El Siglo* are Conservative. Most provincial cities and towns publish their own newspapers and magazines, but it is possible to buy Santafé de Bogotá newspapers in remote Leticia on the day of publication.

A live TV news broadcast

Typical Foods

Tasty snacks like *chorizos*, *empanadas*, *arepas*, and *pasteles de yuca* are found all over Colombia. *Chorizos* are sausages that are usually well seasoned but not spicy. *Empanadas* are pastries filled with meat or chicken, vegetables, and olives, and *arepas* are corn griddle pancakes. *Pasteles de yuca* are pastries made of the flour of a wild tuber called *yuca* and filled with rice, meat, and peas.

Buñuelos, a round sort of doughnut made of corn flour and cheese, are also popular. Fruit salad stands sell *salpicón*, a mixture of finely chopped fruits in orange juice.

Francisco el Hombre

It is said that *vallenato* music was created by Francisco el Hombre. In the days when there was no telephone or newspapers or mail, news was sent from one village to another in the Magdalena River Valley by a sort of town crier. Francisco el Hombre added an accordion and "sang" the news from town to town.

Food for sale at an outdoor market

Regional dishes include *ajiaco de pollo* from Santafé de Bogotá. This potato-based soup is accompanied by chicken, maize, and potato, and served with cream, capers, and chunks of avocado. From Antioquia comes *mazamorra*—boiled maize in milk. Suckling pig is a specialty of Ibagué, and guinea pig is popular in Nariño. Fish is the basic food of the Amazon and Chocó regions.

Soups are often served, especially in the highlands. For breakfast, the main dish is often *changua*, a meat broth with potatoes and freshly chopped cilantro and scallions. *Sopa de pan* is a main-course soup that includes bread, eggs, and cheese. Coffee is served with every meal and at many other times during the day. A small cup of coffee with lots of sugar, known as *tinto*, is a great favorite.

An Ordinary Lunch

Perhaps the dish that comes closest to being the national dish is the *almuerzo corriente*, or *bandeja*, which is a complete lunch and usually not expensive. It begins with a hearty soup followed by rice, potatoes or plantain, a salad, a fried egg, and meat or fish—usually fried—plus beans or lentils. Fresh fruit juice is often included, made from *curuba, maracuya, lulo,* guava, or mango, all local fruits.

Good and plentiful food, cleaner water, better sanitary conditions, and the eradication of some diseases have improved the health of Colombians as a whole. Better medical facilities have curbed infant mortality and help people to live longer.

Just over 40 percent of the people are under 18 years old, but the population is not growing as fast as might be expected. While the average Colombian woman had 5.3 children in 1970, she had 2.7 in 1992. This is largely due to successful family-planning programs.

Colombia's economic potential and its political stability make it better placed than many developing countries to face the next millennium. But politicians must find answers to the guerrilla and drug problems.

A visit to a clinic in Santafé de Bogotá

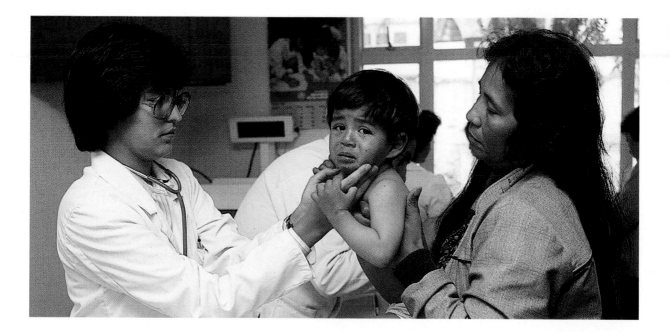

Timeline

Colombian History

Early native people make pottery near what is now Cartagena.	c. 3000 B.C.
Spanish explorers sail along Colombia's Caribbean coast.	A.D. 1500 – 1501
Spaniards found Santa Marta, their first permanent settlement in South America.	1525
Gonzalo Jiménez de Quesada founds Santafé de Bogotá.	1538
The Spanish government creates the *Audiencia* of Santafé de Bogotá.	1549
French pirates attack Cartagena.	1560
Sir Francis Drake destroys much of Cartagena.	1586
Spain creates the Viceroyalty of New Granada, with Santafé de Bogotá as the capital.	1717

World History

c. 2500 B.C.	Egyptians build the Pyramids and Sphinx in Giza.
563 B.C.	Buddha is born in India.
A.D. 313	The Roman emperor Constantine recognizes Christianity.
610	The prophet Muhammad begins preaching a new religion called Islam.
1054	The Eastern (Orthodox) and Western (Roman) Churches break apart.
1066	William the Conqueror defeats the English in the Battle of Hastings.
1095	Pope Urban II proclaims the First Crusade.
1215	King John seals the Magna Carta.
1300s	The Renaissance begins in Italy.
1347	The Black Death sweeps through Europe.
1453	Ottoman Turks capture Constantinople, conquering the Byzantine Empire.
1492	Columbus arrives in North America.
1500s	The Reformation leads to the birth of Protestantism.

Colombian History

Spanish settlers begin a rebellion but are stopped by Spanish forces.	1781
The forces of Simón Bolívar defeat the Spanish at the Battle of Boyacá; Colombia wins its independence.	1819
The state of Gran Colombia is created.	1821
Colombia becomes the Republic of New Granada with control over Panama.	1830
The Republic of the New Granada becomes Colombia.	1863
The War of a Thousand Days between Liberals and Conservatives causes almost 100,000 deaths.	1899 – 1903
Panama gains its independence from Colombia.	1903
President Alfonso López Pumarejo begins social and economic reforms known as the Revolution on the March.	1934 – 1938
La Violencia (violence) between the Liberal and Conservative parties causes about 300,000 deaths.	1948 – 1953; 1954 – 1962
The Liberals and the Conservatives form the National Front.	1958
The National Front ends.	1974
Archaeologists discover the *Ciudad Perdida* (Lost City) of the Tayronas.	1975
Gabriel García Márquez wins the Nobel Prize for literature.	1982
Mount Ruiz erupts and destroys the town of Armero, killing 25,000 people.	1985
The United States government begins helping Colombia to fight the drug runners.	1989
The Constitutional Assembly writes a new constitution for Colombia.	1991
The United States removes Colombia from its list of countries making progress against drug dealers, thus ending U.S. financial aid.	1996

World History

1776	The Declaration of Independence is signed.
1789	The French Revolution begins.
1865	The American Civil War ends.
1914	World War I breaks out.
1917	The Bolshevik Revolution brings Communism to Russia.
1929	Worldwide economic depression begins.
1939	World War II begins, following the German invasion of Poland.
1957	The Vietnam War starts.
1989	The Berlin Wall is torn down as Communism crumbles in Eastern Europe.
1996	Bill Clinton reelected U.S. president.

Fast Facts

Official name: Republic of Colombia

Capital: Santafé de Bogotá, D.C.

Official language: Spanish

Guambiano schoolchildren

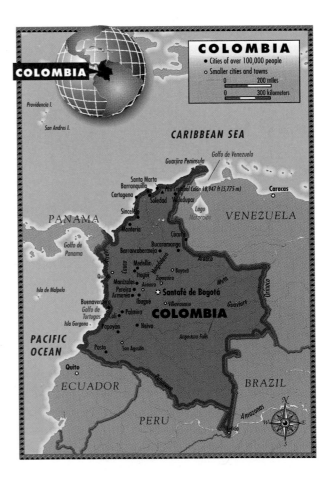

The Colombian flag

An Andean *páramo*

Official religion:	None
Year of founding:	1819
Founder:	Simón Bolívar
National anthem:	Himno Nacional—"Oh Glory Unfading"
Government:	Multiparty republic with two legislative houses—a Senate and a House of Representatives
Chief of state:	President
Area:	439,735 square miles (1,138,826 sq km)
Latitude and longitude of geographic center:	3° 45' N, 73° W
Land and water borders:	Caribbean Sea to the north, Venezuela and Brazil to the east, Peru and Ecuador to the south, Pacific Ocean to the west, and Panama to the northwest
Highest elevation:	Cristóbal Cólon, 18,947 feet (5,775 m) above sea level
Lowest elevation:	Sea level along the coasts
Average temperatures:	58°F (14.4°C) in January in Santafé de Bogotá; 92°F (33.3°C) in July in Cali
Average annual rainfall:	100 inches (254 cm) in the rain forest; 30 inches (76 cm) along the Caribbean Sea
National population (1998 est.):	36,694,000

Population (1996) of largest cities in Colombia:

Santafé deBogotá	6,004,782
Cali	1,985,906
Medellín	1,970,691
Barranquilla	1,157,826
Cartagena	812,595

The Sanctuary of Our Lady of Las Lajas

Famous landmarks:

San Agustín (near Popayán)

Tierradentro (near Popayán)

Fort of San Felipe (outside the walls of Cartagena)

Salt Cathedral (near Zipaquirá)

Sanctuary of Our Lady of Las Lajas (built on a bridge over a river near the Ecuadorean border)

Gold Museum (Santafé de Bogotá)

Lake Guatavita (north of Santafé de Bogotá)

Puracé Volcano National Park (east of Popayán)

Industry: Mining and manufacturing are Colombia's leading industries. Coal and oil are major Colombian exports. About 90 percent of the world's emeralds come from Colombia. Gold and silver are other important mining products. Colombia's major manufactured goods are processed foods and beverages, textiles and clothing, machinery, paper and paper products, and transportation equipment.

Currency: The peso is Colombia's basic monetary unit. Exchange rate, 2003: 2,819 pesos = U.S.$1

Weights and measures: The metric system was introduced in 1857, but Colombians generally use Spanish weights and measures, such as the *vara* (about 28 inches, or 71 cm) and the *arroba* (about 25 pounds, or 11.3 kg).

Literacy: 91 percent (1995 estimate)

Common Spanish words and phrases:

adiós (ah-dee-OHS)	goodbye
arepas (ah-RAY-pahs)	cornmeal pancakes
bambuco (bahm-BOO-koh)	Colombia's national dance
buenos días (BWAHN-ohs DEE-yahs)	good morning
buenas noches (BWAHN-ohs NOH-chess)	good evening/good night

Cumbia dancers

cuánto? (KWAHN-toh)	how much?
cuántos? (KWAHN-tohs)	how many?
Dónde está...? (DOHN-day ess-TAH)	Where is...?
gracias (grah-SEE-ahs)	thank you
hacienda (hah-see-EHN-dah)	a large farm
no (noh)	no
por favor (pohr fah-VOHR)	please
quinoa (ken-OH-ah)	a nutritious cereal native to the high Andes
ruana (roo-AH-nah)	a woolen poncholike garment that opens down the front
sí (see)	yes
vaquero (vah-KEH-roh)	cowboy

Gabriel García Márquez

Famous Colombians:

Fernando Botero *Artist*	(1932–)
Blas de Lezo *Defender of Cartagena*	(c.18th century)
San Pedro Claver *Priest*	(1581–1654)
Gabriel García Márquez *Writer and Nobel Prize winner*	(1932–)
Luis "Lucho" Herrara *Cyclist*	(? – ?)
Carlos Lleras Restrepo *Politician and historian*	(1908–1994)
Rafael Núñez *Politician*	(1825–1894)
Cochise Rodriquez *Cyclist*	(? – ?)
Francisco de Paula Santander *General and politician*	(1792–1840)

To Find Out More

Nonfiction

▶ *Colombia in Pictures.* Visual Geography Series. Minneapolis, Minn.: Lerner Publications, 1987.

▶ Dubois, Jill. *Cultures of the World: Colombia.* Tarrytown, N.Y.: Benchmark Books, 1991.

▶ Dydynski, Krzystof. *Colombia: Travel Survival Kit.*, 2nd ed. Oakland, Calif.: Lonely Planet Publications, 1995.

Fiction

▶ Kendall, Sarita. *Ransom for a River Dolphin.* Minneapolis, Minn.: Lerner Publications, 1993.

Websites

▶ **CIA World Factbook**

http://www.cia.gov/cia/publications/
factbook/geos/co.html

*An excellent overview of the geography,
government, and economy of Colombia*

▶ **Colombia for Kids**

http://www.colombiaemb.org

*Information on Colombia's geography,
natural resources, government, and
economy; maintained by the Embassy
of Colombia*

▶ **Colombia Travel Planner**

http://gosouthamerica.about.com/
library/blindex_Colombia.htm

*Illustrated general background and
tourism information on Colombia*

Organizations and Embassies

▶ Embassy of Colombia
2118 Leroy Place, N.W.
Washington, D.C. 20008
(202) 387-8338

Index

Page numbers in *italics* indicate illustrations.

Meet the Author

MARION MORRISON studied history in college and first traveled widely in Colombia in the 1960s. She lived in Santafé de Bogotá and in the country near Cartagena. Her extensive travels in South America since then have enabled her to return to Colombia frequently. She is fascinated with the country's often romantic past. "It is not easy to miss the depth of feeling that Colombians have for their heritage. They project their feelings with a passion grown from the liberation of South America.

"My research for this book began with the diaries and notes I have kept from my travels. Some of the aspects I recall vividly from photographs and news clippings I have gathered. For instance, I was in Santafé de Bogotá for the historic visit by Pope Paul VI in 1968. At that time, Colombia was the most strongly Catholic country of any I had visited in South America, yet the first birth control clinics were beginning to appear. On another occasion, my zoologist husband and I went high in the *páramos* flanking the Puracé Volcano to follow the footsteps of the early scientific travelers. We have seen the illegal slaughter of turtles on the beaches of the north coast.

"At home we have a library of books about and from South and Central America, which I use all the time, and we have access to a fine collection in central London. We are members of several organizations involved with Latin America, and over the years we have made many friends in the area. These days, using e-mail it is inexpensive and very quick to check on facts, and luckily most of our friends respond quickly."

Photo Credits